BEAR

ALSO BY ROBERT GREENFIELD

❧

Ain't It Time We Said Goodbye:
The Rolling Stones on the Road to Exile

Anyone Who Had a Heart:
My Life and Music (with Burt Bacharach)

The Last Sultan:
The Life and Times of Ahmet Ertegun

A Day in the Life:
One Family, the Beautiful People, and the End of the Sixties

Exile on Main Street:
A Season in Hell with the Rolling Stones

Timothy Leary: A Biography

Dark Star: An Oral Biography of Jerry Garcia

Bill Graham Presents:
My Life Inside Rock and Out (with Bill Graham)

Temple (novel)

Haymon's Crowd (novel)

The Spiritual Supermarket:
An Account of Gurus Gone Public in America

S.T.P.:
A Journey Through America with the Rolling Stones

Robert Greenfield

BEAR

The Life and Times of
Augustus Owsley Stanley III

THOMAS DUNNE BOOKS
St. Martin's Press
New York

THOMAS DUNNE BOOKS.
An imprint of St. Martin's Press.

BEAR. Copyright © 2016 by Robert Greenfield. All rights reserved.
Printed in the United States of America. For information, address
St. Martin's Press, 175 Fifth Avenue, New York, N.Y. 10010.

www.thomasdunnebooks.com
www.stmartins.com

Designed by Kathryn Parise

The Library of Congress Cataloging-in-Publication Data
is available upon request.

ISBN 978-1-250-08121-6 (hardcover)
ISBN 978-1-4668-9311-5 (e-book)

Our books may be purchased in bulk for promotional, educational, or
business use. Please contact your local bookseller or the Macmillan Corporate
and Premium Sales Department at 1-800-221-7945, extension 5442, or by
e-mail at MacmillanSpecialMarkets@macmillan.com.

First Edition: November 2016

10 9 8 7 6 5 4 3 2 1

For Donna, and for Shelley, for everything

Contents

I'm not interested in having a biography of any kind published about me or any mention of my childhood. Anything written about me should be about the things I've done and the skills and talents I have and not, "He grew up here, he went to this school, he was in trouble there," and all that bullshit. Because that's the way you create celebrityhood and I'm not into being a celebrity. I don't give a shit.

—Augustus Owsley Stanley III, aka Bear,
January 31, 2007

❧

There's nothing wrong with Bear that a few billion less brain cells wouldn't cure.

—Jerry Garcia

BEAR

Prologue

The Muir Beach Acid Test

❧〜❀〜❧

Amid all the swirling madness being created by Ken Kesey and his band of Merry Pranksters in the Muir Beach Lodge on Saturday, December 11, 1965, one thing is eminently clear. The guy who supplied all the high-octane rocket fuel powering this event is definitely freaking out. Everyone knows this because for what feels like hours but has only been about ten or fifteen minutes, he has been making the most horrible screeching and scraping noises imaginable by dragging an old wooden chair back and forth across the floor.

Had he been doing this at one of the wedding receptions that regularly take place here in this hundred-foot log cabin, someone would already have long since asked him to stop. Because this is an Acid Test where everyone is tripping on LSD and there are no rules, no one is about to do anything about it even though the sound is driving everybody up the proverbial wall.

On every level imaginable, the guy has already had himself quite an evening. Having never before taken acid with the Pranksters, he has seen the Grateful Dead perform for the first time. Accompanied by a flashing strobe, a light machine, and a home movie that was being shown by two projectors at once, the sound of Jerry Garcia's lead guitar wrapped itself around the guy's mind like the claws of a tiger.

Initially terrified, he then had the stunning revelation that would shape the rest of his life. The Grateful Dead are not just good. They are fantastic. Someday, they are going to be even bigger than the Beatles. Although the guy has no idea how he can help them accomplish this goal, what he wants to do now is to hitch a ride with the most amazing group he has ever seen and somehow make a positive contribution to their future.

While all this might already have been more than enough for anyone else, the LSD he has taken combined with the weirdness of the Pranksters' current sound interval suddenly mesh to send him off somewhere that he has never before been. Losing all control of his body, he finds himself trapped in an endless spiral of utterly fantastic scenes.

As Tom Wolfe will later write in *The Electric Kool-Aid Acid Test*, this guy has now been transported back to the eighteenth century, where he sees himself as an "alchemist, seer, magician, master of precognition, forecaster of lotteries" stuck in a dank dungeon in the Bastille, which itself then shatters into fragments as he loses all of his skin and then his entire skeleton as well. With "his whole substance dissolving into gaseous nothingness," he becomes a single cell.

"One human cell: his; that was all that was left of the entire known world and if he lost control of that one cell, there would be nothing left. The world would be, like, over."

Making the guy's current plight yet even more dire, one of the Pranksters geometrically increases his paranoia by pointing out some conventionally dressed guests who might well be the police. Although LSD is still legal in California, the guy is holding so much of it at the moment that he decides the time has come for him to split the scene and get the hell out of here just as fast as he possibly can.

Running out the door, he leaps behind the wheel of his car and begins driving madly along the narrow, winding road leading away from the Muir Beach Lodge. In no condition to drive, much less do anything else, he promptly runs his car into a ditch. Abandoning the vehicle, he charges back into the lodge and does something that is completely unthinkable on every level imaginable by confronting the unbelievably powerful and incredibly charismatic Ken Kesey about what is going on here tonight.

In no uncertain terms, the guy tells the noted author of *One Flew Over the Cuckoo's Nest*, who is also the peerless and unchallenged leader of the Merry Pranksters, that he and his cohorts are messing around with something they do not understand. Taking LSD in this kind of wildly out-of-control group situation in order to awaken the part of the unconscious mind that used to be defined as containing all of the angels and devils is extremely dangerous. And since it is the guy's LSD that made all this happen, he is going to ensure that tonight's Acid Test will be the last one ever held by cutting off their supply.

Laughing off everything that the guy is saying to him, Kesey responds to the diatribe by pinning a badge on the guy's shirt.

Precisely why Kesey has chosen to do this, no one knows. Offended by the act, the guy's girlfriend promptly removes the badge, only to have Kesey take it away from her. In true Prankster fashion, Kesey says, "No, no. He gets to decide if he wants to wear it or not." And then puts the badge right back on the guy's shirt.

Due to the overwhelming popularity of *The Electric Kool-Aid Acid Test,* Tom Wolfe's account of this freak-out soon becomes the stuff of legend. In the book, Wolfe, who himself had never taken LSD, somehow manages to convey the all-out careening madness that acid can sometimes induce even in the mind of not just the most experienced user but also someone whom Grateful Dead bassist Phil Lesh will later describe as "the Johnny Appleseed of LSD."

As the man in question, born Augustus Owsley Stanley III but then known to one and all simply as Owsley, will later say, "The Pranksters were playing around with Wolfe and he didn't have a clue. He didn't realize who and what they were. Nothing about me in that book was accurate. It was what other people said about me. I never met Wolfe and the man never talked to me. So it was all his fantasy about it or someone else's fantasy about it."

But then in the world according to Augustus Owsley Stanley III, only he was ever right all the time.

1

Bluegrass Roots

❧

In a state where politics was right up there with Thoroughbred horse racing as the sport of choice, and extremely colorful and vitriolic campaigns for local political office always seemed to be going on, if only to provide Kentuckians with "an excellent excuse for having community picnics, fried chicken dinners, and fish fries," Augustus Owsley Stanley was an authentically larger-than-life figure whom his grandson would later describe as "the last of the great silver throated Southern orators."

Born on May 21, 1867, in Shelbyville, Kentucky, Nuddicut Owsley Stanley was ten years old when he persuaded his parents to change his given name to Augustus after his maternal grandmother, Augusta Stanley, so that he would never be referred as No Stanley. For wildly different reasons, one hundred years later Augustus Owsley Stanley III would follow in his grandfather's footsteps by also changing his name to suit his particular needs.

On both sides of his family, A. O. Stanley's lineage was impressive. During the Civil War, his father, William Stanley, had served as a captain in the Orphan Brigade of the Confederate Army, a unit commanded by Major General John C. Breckinridge, who had been the youngest vice president in US history. After having worked as the associate editor of the *Shelby Sentinel*, William Stanley became a Campbellite minister. A. O. Stanley's mother, Amanda Rodes Owsley, was the niece of former Kentucky governor William Owsley, after whom the state's Owsley County was named.

In 1885, A. O. Stanley entered the Kentucky Agricultural and Mechanical College in Lexington. After graduating from Centre College in 1887, he served as chair of belles lettres at Christian College in Hustonville, and then as the principal of Marion Academy in Bradfordsville and Mackville Academy in Mackville, while studying law at night. Admitted to the state bar in 1894, he began practicing in Flemingsburg, where his father served as the minister of a local church.

Moving to Henderson with less than $100 in his pocket, A. O. Stanley established a thriving law practice and began campaigning for Democratic candidates in local elections. In 1900, he was named an elector for William Jennings Bryan, who was then defeated in the presidential election by William McKinley.

Two years later at the age of thirty-five, A. O. Stanley was elected to Congress from Kentucky's Second District. He then married Susan Soaper, whose father was a prominent figure in the state's tobacco industry. A laissez-faire progressive and a disciple of Thomas Jefferson, A. O. Stanley fought to end the federal tax on tobacco. After President William Howard Taft called a special session of Congress to repeal the tariff, what became known as the Stanley Bill was passed into law.

While serving as chairman of the congressional commission charged with trust busting, Stanley sponsored and then conducted an investigation into the monopolistic business practices of the US Steel Corporation and introduced three antitrust bills that eventually led to the passage of the Clayton Act. After he had been reelected to Congress in 1912, Stanley entered the Kentucky senatorial campaign on a pro-liquor platform, but was defeated in the Democratic primary.

In 1915, he ran for governor against Republican Edwin P. Morrow. Appearing together day after day throughout the state during the campaign, the two men attacked one another relentlessly in public but soon became good friends who often drank together after having debated one another. Indicating that he may have had a bit too much fondness for Kentucky bourbon, A. O. Stanley got to his feet to speak one day after his opponent had already addressed the crowd only to stagger to the back of the stage so he could throw up. Returning to the stand, he said, "Gentlemen, I beg you to forgive me. Every time I hear Ed Morrow speak, it makes me sick to my stomach." A. O. Stanley won the election by 471 votes.

As governor of Kentucky, Stanley vetoed a bill designed to prohibit the teaching of German in Kentucky schools during World War I while saying, "We are at war with an armed despotism, not a language." He also enacted the state's first workman's compensation law, passed antitrust statutes, and improved Kentucky's charitable, penal, and educational institutions.

In January 1917, Stanley made national news by preventing the

lynching of a black prisoner, a circuit court judge, and a Commonwealth of Kentucky attorney in Murray, Kentucky. Before boarding the night train to travel there from Lexington, the state capital,
he boldly proclaimed, "I shall give the mob a chance to lynch the
governor of Kentucky first." He then defused the situation by going
to where the judge and the Commonwealth attorney were being
held hostage and daring to mob to kill him.

In 1918, Stanley was elected as the junior senator from the state
of Kentucky. A strong supporter of women's suffrage and the League
of Nations, he consistently denounced laws that limited individual
freedom and was once quoted as saying, "You cannot milk a cow in
America without a federal inspector at your heels." He was also frequently mentioned as a Democratic candidate to succeed Wood-
row Wilson as president.

Throughout his political career in a state that considered itself
the birthplace of bourbon whiskey, A. O. Stanley had always been
dogged by his pro-liquor position. At a time when Prohibition was
seen by many Americans as the only cure for a wide variety of social problems, Kentucky voters had narrowly approved a state con-
stitutional amendment banning the sale and distribution of alcohol
two months before the Volstead Act established Prohibition as the
law of the land in 1920.

Unable to counter the powerful opposition mounted against
him by the Anti-Saloon League as well as the Ku Klux Klan, A. O.
Stanley was defeated in his bid for reelection to the Senate in 1924
by more than twenty-four thousand votes. Despite his progressive
views on a wide variety of issues, his career as an elected official
came to a sudden halt, primarily because of his stance on a substance that was now illegal in America. In time, his grandson

would suffer far harsher consequences for synthesizing and distributing a far more powerful substance that also allowed individuals to alter their consciousness.

After leaving office, A. O. Stanley resumed his law practice in Washington, DC, and Louisville. In 1930, he was appointed by President Herbert Hoover to the International Joint Commission. During his twenty-four years of service on the commission, A. O. Stanley ardently supported the creation of the Saint Lawrence Seaway. After a period of declining health, he died at the age of ninety-one in 1958. After his flag-draped casket had laid in state in the Capitol Rotunda, A. O. Stanley was buried in Frankfort Cemetery near other former governors of Kentucky.

Born on July 1, 1904, his son Augustus Owsley Stanley Jr. was eleven years old when his father was elected governor. At the age of fourteen, A. O. Stanley Jr. moved with his family to Washington, DC. Three years later, he served as a clerk to his father at a salary of $1,500 a year. A. O. Stanley Jr. then entered the Naval Academy.

As his son would later say, "He did not graduate. He flaked out in his plebe year because he had a bad sinus condition, which I think was as much psychosomatic as anything else. I think he was a fragile personality and was too proud to go back and do his plebe year all over again because he had only completed one full semester. After the Naval Academy, he went to engineering school, but he didn't finish that either."

Apparently seeking some sort of career that would allow him to emerge from the shadow of his father's outsized personality, A. O. Stanley Jr. went to work as a surveyor for the Chesapeake and Ohio Railroad. In his son's words, "Then the Depression came along and they stopped maintaining the rails and began laying off staff. About that time, he met my mother and got married."

On June 24, 1933, A. O. Stanley Jr. married Lella Lane Ray of Richmond, Virginia, in Henderson, Kentucky. Taking up residence in Washington, DC, the couple enjoyed an active social life centered around high-level Democratic Party functions as well as festive gatherings sponsored by the Kentucky Society.

A. O. Stanley Jr. then began working as a clerk in the Reconstruction Finance Corporation, a federal agency founded in 1932 to provide aid to state and local governments while also making loans to banks, railroads, and mortgage associations. After President Franklin Delano Roosevelt took office in March 1933, the agency's funding and powers were greatly expanded as part of the New Deal and A. O. Stanley Jr. was most likely hired by the agency during this period.

It also seems likely that his father's long-standing friendship with Stanley Forman Reed, a well-known lawyer who had served in the Kentucky General Assembly before representing the Chesapeake and Ohio Railroad and was then serving as general counsel of the Reconstruction Finance Corporation, made it possible for A. O. Stanley Jr. to obtain both of these jobs with those organizations. Reed, who became a Supreme Court justice in 1938, was also the godfather of Augustus Owsley Stanley III.

After having attended Colombus Law School, A. O. Stanley Jr. was granted a legal degree. In 1936, he was admitted without examination to the Kentucky State bar. As his son would later say, "He transferred into the legal department of the Reconstruction Finance department and continued working there through all of its changes for the next thirty-three or thirty-four years until after it turned into the Small Business Administration."

Despite being thirty-seven years old when the United States entered World War II in 1941, A. O. Stanley Jr. enlisted in the Navy. As his son would later say, "What happened was that with his one year at the Naval Academy, they sent him to Officer Candidate School and he got commissioned as a second lieutenant. He was working in intelligence and he was very good at it, but he wanted to go fight, so he finagled a transfer to the Pacific and wound up being attached to an admiral's staff. The admiral was on the USS Lexington during the Battle of the Coral Sea, and the *Lexington* was literally blown up from underneath them."

Intent on capturing Port Moresby in New Guinea, the last Allied base between Japan and Australia, three Japanese fleets comprised of two large aircraft carriers, a smaller carrier, two heavy cruisers, as well as supporting craft set sail for New Guinea and the Solomon Islands during the first week in May 1942. After having been alerted to the operation by radio intercepts, three large groups of US Navy vessels moved to oppose the Japanese fleets. The resulting battle was the first naval engagement in history in which the opposing ships neither saw nor ever fired directly upon one another.

At 1113 hours on May 8, 1942, the USS *Lexington,* one of the US Navy's oldest aircraft carriers, was attacked by Japanese Nakajima B5N torpedo bombers. At 1120 hours, the first torpedo hit the ship and exploded near the port forward gun gallery. A minute later, another torpedo struck near the bridge. A one-thousand-pound bomb dropped by an Aichi D3A dive bomber then hit the ready-ammunition locker close to Admiral Aubrey Fitch's cabin. The

Lexington was then hit by two more bombs, injuring and killing crew members who were manning the ship's machine guns and aft signal station.

In all, the *Lexington* was rocked by seventeen separate explosions. As fire began spreading throughout the vessel, the ship started listing to port. At 1247 hours, gasoline vapor that had accumulated from leaking fuel tanks belowdecks ignited. The huge explosion that followed proved to be the killing blow. As the *Lexington*'s commanding officer, Captain Frederick C. Sherman, would later write in his report, "From this point on, the ship was doomed."

At 1630 hours as the fires burned out of control, the *Lexington* came to a dead stop in the water. Admiral Fitch directed the USS *Morris* to come alongside, and personnel began disembarking from the *Lexington* by going down lines onto the deck of the destroyer. At 1707 hours, Admiral Fitch issued the order to abandon ship. Crew members went hand over hand down lines into life rafts. In accordance with naval tradition, Admiral Fitch and Captain Sherman were the last to leave the bridge. Both officers were then taken by whaleboat to the USS *Minneapolis*.

As Sherman would later write, "The picture of the burning and doomed ship was a magnificent but sad sight. The ship and crew had performed gloriously and it seemed too bad that she had to perish in her hour of victory." In all, 216 crewmen on the USS *Lexington* were killed in the Battle of the Coral Sea. Miraculously, 2,375 men, A. O. Stanley Jr. among them, survived.

In his son's words, "My father must have seen the most horrible warfare imaginable. There were nearly three thousand men on this huge aircraft carrier loaded with high explosives and high-octane petrol and the Japanese were dropping bombs on it and firing torpedoes at it and crew members were being burned and blown to bits.

"It just fucked with his head and he became a lifelong alcoholic. The worst kind of alcoholic I ever saw in my life. I don't know if he was in the water after the *Lexington* was hit because he would never talk about it. Never. Not a word. After the war ended, he transferred into the Naval Reserve and attended a meeting every Tuesday night for the next twenty years or so and then retired with a double pension—the Navy and the United States government—and he managed to drink it all up every day.

"He was magnificently dwarfed by his own father. My father was twenty percent smarter than me, but my grandfather was more than twenty percent smarter than him. He had one of the most awesome minds I've ever known in my entire life. My experience of my grandfather was as an old man and I loved him. He had the greatest stories and all the greatest books and he could quote something and then tell me where to find that quote, and he was right every time. He didn't believe in much government regulation but he really believed in the common man."

As his father was still working as a government clerk while going to law school at night during the heart of the Depression, Augustus Owsley Stanley III was born on January 19, 1935. As he would later note, "My name is not Augustus Owsley Stanley III, the leaden sobriquet I was saddled with at birth. That was my grandfather and my father's name. My dad suffered the awful brand 'Junior,' the poor bastard, and I have never considered that I am a 'third' anything.

"I so resented the media claiming I was playing on my grandfather's 'famous' name that I had it legally changed by court order in 1967 to simply 'Owsley Stanley,' which is all I was ever called during my early life anyway. I hated 'Gus' like poison—the usual nickname for 'Augustus'—and to this day, I do not understand why anyone would saddle one of their children with someone else's name plus a number."

By then, the epic generational battle between the son and grandson of a man who had been authentic bluegrass political royalty was already raging as fiercely as the fires that had destroyed the USS *Lexington* during the Battle of the Coral Sea.

Growing Up Absurd

Whatever marital problems A. O. Stanley Jr. and his wife might have been having before he enlisted in the Navy and went off to fight in the Pacific seem to have only been made worse by his extended tour of duty overseas. In 1943, Lella Stanley decided to separate from her husband. She then ended their ten-year marriage by divorcing him. With both her eight-year-old son Augustus and his six-year-old brother in tow, she moved to Los Angeles, where her sister lived. In later years, what Owsley would remember best about his mother was that she loved to play the violin and piano while singing in the key of C. Never as musically talented as her, he took violin lessons but was unable to "quite get the knack" of the instrument. Although he also liked to sing as a boy, he left the choir after his voice changed.

An extraordinarily gifted but difficult child who while living in Virginia had been raised in great part by "black nannies whom we always treated very well," Owsley had somehow managed to teach himself to read at the age of two and a half by studying comic books.

As he later told Bruce Eisner, "I didn't recognize letters; I read more or less like the Chinese would. . . . The word itself was like a picture. It had a shape, the shape was composed of the strokes; the strokes, of course, were the letters. I didn't know a letter could be interpreted separately. It took me a long time to learn to use the dictionary successfully because I couldn't make any sense out of a sequence for the alphabet. It was just a bunch of strokes."

At school, Owsley was neither a willing nor a cooperative student. "I didn't like the bullshit," he would later say. "I wanted to learn and read things and do other interesting stuff, and they wanted me to play ring-around-the-rosie in sixth grade. I thought recess was my time off and I should be able to do what I wanted, read or make drawings, rather than run around the yard. So I got into a lot of trouble."

When he was eleven years old, his mother decided she could no longer cope with her firstborn son and sent him back East to live with his father. By then, A. O. Stanley Jr. was married to his second wife, the former Callie Mullen Reese of Fredericksburg, Virginia. She had brought to the marriage a daughter, who was now eleven years old, and a son, who was nine. Owsley treated his stepbrother "like dog shit. I was the older one but he was too close to me in age and I had no real relationship with him at all. I was getting dumped on and so I then dumped it all on him."

To instill some discipline in his own son and alleviate the growing tension in his home, Owsley's father placed him in Charlotte Hall Military Academy. Located in Charlotte Hall, Maryland, about forty miles from where his father and stepmother were now living in Alexandria, Virginia, the school had been established in 1774 by England's Queen Charlotte "to provide for the liberal and pious education of youth to better fit them for the discharge of their duties for the British Empire."

One of the oldest educational institutions in the United States, Charlotte Hall comprised several colonial-style buildings scattered across more than three hundred acres of rolling land. Decked out in full military uniforms replete with Sam Browne belts, the all-male student body was so small that a typical graduating class consisted of just twenty-four members.

The only lasting lesson that Owsley seems to have learned at Charlotte Hall was imparted to him by his boxing coach. In what was then considered an unorthodox practice, the coach would not allow his team to eat breakfast on the day of a match. An hour before their bouts began, each member of the team was given a steak without any salt on it to eat but was not allowed to drink water.

"The result was, of course, was that it was digested and all that energy was circulating around our system, all the fat and protein and everything else was all in our blood. There was nothing left in our gut so we could take pounding on our gut, no worries, and we had an enormous amount of power and endurance. It worked!" Throughout his adult life, Owsley would adhere so strictly to an all-meat diet that it soon became one of his defining characteristics. At Charlotte Hall, he also acquired the nickname that would stay with him for the rest of his life. Because of his hairy chest, he became known as Bear.

Although the headmaster of Charlotte Hall would later describe Owsley as "almost like a brainchild, a wunderkinder, tremendously interested in science," he also remembered him as being willful and wild. "I was tossed out of the military academy not because I was a poor student. I was one of the top students in the school. I was tossed out because of this rogue, get-high nature of mine. I managed to smuggle some kind of alcohol into that school for every single student, and the entire student body was blasted out of their minds at this sort of homecoming weekend. I kind of stumbled down the stairs and got caught."

While there is no knowing how he obtained enough alcohol to get the entire student body at Charlotte Hall Military Academy drunk, Owsley was then in ninth grade and so small in stature that it seems doubtful he could have purchased it legally. Although it is impossible to know whether he had stolen all this liquor from his father, Owsley did get himself expelled by providing his fellow students with the substance that had already permanently altered his relationship with his father.

After returning home to live with his father and stepmother, Owsley began attending Washington-Lee High School in Arlington, Virginia, where he often ate at the same table in the cafeteria as Shirley MacLaine, the well-known actress, who was then a year ahead of him at the school. In 1950, when he was fifteen years old, Owsley accepted what must have been a proposal that his father had offered him and allowed himself to be admitted as a voluntary patient at St. Elizabeth's Hospital, a psychiatric institution in Southeastern Washington, DC. That he was willing to do so speaks volumes about how intolerable his living situation must have become at home.

Designed in part by the social activist Dorothea Dix, what was then known as the Government Hospital for the Insane had opened its doors in January 1855. Located on more than 350 acres on a plateau in the nation's capital, the institution helped develop standards of care for mentally ill patients in state hospitals throughout America. At its peak during the mid-1940s, 7,450 patients were housed in the hospital's 130 buildings.

After the world-renowned poet Ezra Pound had been brought back from Italy in 1945 and charged with treason for having called for the assassination of President Franklin D. Roosevelt while also espousing anti-Semitic views during radio broadcasts made for the Axis powers during World War II, he was also confined in St. Elizabeth's Hospital. When Pound was finally released from the institution after having spent twelve years there, he was asked his opinion of his native country. Pound's succinct response was "All America is an insane asylum."

Despite the dark and distinctly foreboding nature of some of the older parts of the institution, Owsley seems to have felt far more content during his fifteen-month stay at St. Elizabeth's than he had ever been in his father's home. "I don't know if I was having a nervous breakdown. I was just a neurotic kid. My mother died a few months into the experience. She was washing her car and collapsed and died of a heart attack. But it was there that I sorted out my guilt problems about everything, and I came out of it pretty clear.

"They didn't do much of anything to me there because with neurotics, it was therapy. But the talking didn't work. It wasn't until they gave me a therapist who used hypnosis and psychodrama in this little room with a stage and colored lights that things started to change for me. The hypnosis was interesting because I learned the tricks of self-hypnosis. Going to sleep is a little like hypnosis. If you do something with your mind, you can go to sleep in about a minute. And I can do that. I can sleep anywhere at any time."

Although "it totally freaked out the staff," Owsley soon discovered that he could use a bedspring to pry open doors, thereby enabling him to leave the institution whenever he liked. "If I did something bad, they would send me to the top ward, and I'd work my way back down to the bottom again. But all along, I knew that not only could I walk up to the admissions clerk and say, 'I'm tired of being here, turn me loose,' but I could also go for a walk at night because I could let myself in and out. I didn't do that a lot, but I could."

After having established his mastery of the system in which he now found himself, Owsley came to the somewhat stunning realization that none of this was his fault. "It was hard for me to break free because my parents were a couple of assholes. Neither one of them really wanted to be parents. They had no skills whatsoever at it. All I know is that I felt really shortchanged in parenting, and that caused me a lot of guilt. If you feel you can't love someone whom you are universally told that you must love, you become very guilty. 'What's wrong with me? I can't seem to love these people.'

"Any animal can have offspring, but that doesn't have anything to do with their competency in managing their upbringing or anything else. It's a happenstance of nature. Once I realized this, that freed me. It's too bad I missed out on that loving parental care, but I learned that I couldn't blame myself for it."

After he was released from St. Elizabeth's Hospital, Owsley returned home to live with his father and stepmother and once again began attending Washington-Lee High School. "And then, the school system punished me by not allowing me to take a test and go back into the proper class. They set me a year behind, and by the time I was in eleventh grade, I'd had my fill of high school and all that bullshit."

Despite having achieved the highest score on the achievement test in physics ever reported by the school, he had by then already been given a D in the subject by "an incompetent very senior female teacher who was only there because of tenure" for pointing out that she had contradicted the textbook.

Without having ever graduated from high school, Owsley was then admitted to the School of Engineering at the University of Virginia. Because he thought engineers actually made things and one of his great childhood heroes had always been Dr. Elias Huer, the genius who helped Buck Rogers in one of the comic strips Owsley had loved as a boy, "I picked engineering. But it was a bad choice because I really didn't like things like surveying and heavy mechanical drawing. I hated slide rules so badly that this alone would have prevented me from ever working as an engineer."

Founded in Charlottesville, Virginia, in 1819 by Thomas Jefferson, who himself had attended the College of William and Mary, the University of Virginia was a publicly funded institution that in many ways more closely resembled an elite Ivy League college. Social life on its sprawling campus dotted with historically significant buildings that Jefferson had initially designed centered on a variety of powerful secret societies. These groups were then supplanted by numerous fraternities and other societies, to which about a third of the student body still belong.

Despite his somewhat impressive lineage, Owsley fit in no better at the University of Virginia than he had anywhere else. "I was the kind of guy who never took notes when I was in college. I would buy my textbooks, read them all through, and then sell them all back to the bookstore during the first week of the course at full price as if I'd changed classes. I had a scary kind of memory and never needed to look at them again. I never took notes but I was getting B-pluses and I had three-point-four average. My father wouldn't support me when I went to college because I had not graduated from high school, and so I wasn't able to do it for long."

Dropping out of the University of Virginia after a year, Owsley returned home. At the age of eighteen, he had the classic 1950s confrontation with his father over what was then the ultimate symbol of adolescent rebellion—a motorcycle. "I was terrified of leaving home, yet I had to because my father was so controlling that he insisted he would not allow me to have a motorcycle. He said he would take my license, and I said, 'You have nothing to do with my license. I'm eighteen!' He said, 'If you don't follow my instructions, I don't want you in my house. Get out!'

"He just said it in anger, but I grabbed my stuff and jumped in my car and drove to see my grandmother in Washington. She knew my father and I were diametrically opposed and had told me when I was younger that if I ever had any problems, I was welcome to come live with them. Which I did, and I never lived in my father's house again."

Twelve years later, in April 1965, Owsley showed up in Alexandria, Virginia, with Melissa Cargill, who was then his girlfriend. Four miles from home, he called his father, but the two soon began to argue over the phone. After Owsley had informed his father that booze was far worse than drugs, A. O. Stanley Jr. told his son to wash his hands and then come back to talk to him.

Calling his son "emotionally unbalanced" while acknowledging that he also had "a brilliant mind," A. O. Stanley Jr. told a reporter from the *Los Angeles Times*, "We haven't had a pleasant relationship. We're not in accord with what he's doing. His life is divorced from ours. He's had two wives and a child by each and lives with another woman. When he came here with that floozy, I wouldn't let him in."

The two men then did not speak to one another again for five years. In what even now seems like an antebellum response to their falling out, Owsley would later say, "He had insulted Melissa by referring to her in speaking to me as a 'hussy'—an antique Southern derogatory term taken to mean 'common as dirt and lacking morals.' I waited in vain for his apology. He wrote me when I was in jail and indicated he wished to repair the break. I did not bring up the insulting terminology and so far as I can remember, he never spoke negatively about her again."

With his son having already become an authentic legend in the counterculture, A. O. Stanley Jr., who was then sixty-three years old and retired, announced in March 1968 that he intended to run in the Kentucky Democratic US senatorial primary by stating that "an old name with a new face might be attractive" to voters. One of fourteen candidates in the race, he garnered just 621 votes, thereby putting an end to his nascent political career.

Owsley Stanley's stepmother died on May 26, 1978. Owsley Stanley's father, who had attained the rank of commander in the Naval Reserve, passed away on September 4, 1979, at the age of seventy-five. Beneath a single stone at Arlington National Cemetery in Virginia, the two are interred together.

3

Shape-Shifting

~⧫~

Still living with his grandparents in Washington, DC, Owsley spent the summer when he was nineteen years old working as a lifeguard at a pool in Bethesda, Maryland. While doing a "clown dive" that some Hawaiian guys in the military were trying to teach him, Owsley hit the water so hard that he suffered a middle-ear hemorrhage, which then became infected. "It was my right ear and it did something to my hearing. Both ears have an entirely different character. All the highs would come in through my left ear, which is connected to the right brain, where most art and creativity come from so I've been developing my right brain since I was nineteen."

The way Owsley's hearing was affected eventually shaped the way in which he would record bands as they performed onstage. "When I got into sound and began taking acid, I developed a remarkable facility insofar as my hearing was concerned that intensified my art. I do hear in stereo, and I absolutely hear the separation, but pan pots do not move the sound for me. A stereo record done with pan pots sounds to me like a mono record. I have to put on headphones to make any difference at all, and then it's still blurry, so I don't ever put a single source into both channels. There's always a second microphone, and if I want a single source in both channels, I use two because I'm only interested in differences and my ears do know that."

At some point after that summer, Owsley moved to Los Angeles, where he began working as a rocket-test engineer for Rocketdyne, a newly formed division of North American Aviation that was then designing and manufacturing the Navaho intercontinental cruise missile. In June 1956, Owsley enlisted in the US Air Force. After somehow managing to survive eight and half weeks of basic training, he was assigned to the Rocket Engine Test Facility at Edwards Air Force Base in Antelope Valley in the western Mojave Desert.

"I wound up teaching myself electronics, which I knew nothing about. I was reassigned to the salvage yard and took apart every piece of gear that came in—and there was some pretty high-tech stuff at Edwards." During Owsley's time in the Air Force, he also passed the tests for both his ham radio and First Class Radiotelephone Operator's licenses.

Discharged after eighteen months for reasons that may have had something to do with his unwillingness to adjust to military life, Owsley returned to Los Angeles and began working at various Southern California radio and TV stations, including a stint as chief engineer at an AM station in San Diego.

"I was twenty-three and all kinds of things were going on in Los Angeles, but I couldn't get a regular job as a broadcast engineer because of the union, so I had to work summer relief. I'd make three or four hundred dollars a week, which in those days was a lot of money. I'd save it all up and live as frugally as I could, and then during the rest of the year, I'd draw unemployment and go to school."

During this period, Owsley attended Los Angeles City College. He was also arrested after being caught with a fourteen-year-old girl in a motel room, but was released after being given a lecture by the judge. In May 1959, Owsley went to the Shrine Auditorium to see the Bolshoi Ballet perform on their groundbreaking eight-week tour that generated widespread public attention in America for ballet.

"I was very impressed with Vladimir Vasiliev. I would say he was the most remarkable dancer I'd ever seen in my life. He made Baryshnikov and the rest of those guys look like amateurs. He did things I did not think were humanly possible. And then I tried to talk to him and he couldn't speak English, so I decided to study Russian and ballet. I went down and signed up to do both, and I stayed with it for about six years. I was taking two ballet classes a day five days a week, each about an hour and a half long, so I was way overtrained. I should have started when I was eleven or twelve when I first came across ballet and thought it was fascinating, but I hadn't.

"For the last couple of years that I was into it, I did little parts in local companies, but I knew by then that although I really loved it, there was no way I could ever develop the kind of skill I would have needed. I didn't have the turnout. I didn't have the point. I had the strength. I had tremendous elevation. Probably because of my diet. That was how I got on it. I couldn't dance and eat a mixed diet, so I switched to meat and everything was fine."

In 1961, Owsley married a girl from La Cañada, California, in a ceremony in Tijuana that turned out to be invalid. She gave birth to a son named Peter, but the marriage ended a year later when Owsley left her. He then married another woman with whom he had a daughter, named Nina, but the two were soon divorced as well. One of his ex-wives would later call him "just a little boy afraid to grow up—a Peter Pan."

Returning to Daytona Beach, Florida, where he had lived with his first wife, Owsley was arrested on a charge of disorderly conduct in 1963. The police returned him to Los Angeles, where he was wanted for having written $645 in bad checks. As part of a plea bargain designed to keep him from going to jail, Owsley informed the judge that he now intended to turn over a brand-new leaf in his life by returning to college to earn his degree. He was given a six-month suspended sentence, fined $250, and placed on three years' probation.

Having learned a lesson that he never forgot, Owsley then began conducting all of his business transactions in cash. "I bounced some checks and got into trouble, and I realized I couldn't deal with the regular, commercial form of finance. . . . I regretted it. I thought it was a terrible breach of honor and everything else on my part; I was just appalled at what I had done. The judge gave me probation, and when the probation ended, I sort of felt like I had been released from something."

By any standard known to man, Owsley Stanley to this point in his life could only have been described as an oddball, a weirdo, and an eccentric. In many ways, his life had followed a classic fifties paradigm—the loner, the outsider, the rebel without a cause who knew only that everything he had been offered so far did not suit his needs and that no matter how hard he tried, he would always be an extremely square peg in a very round hole.

All that changed when Owsley moved to Berkeley in 1964 to take classes at the University of California. In a city where the counterculture in America was then already beginning to be born, he found the calling that would eventually transform him into a man of power whose name then become known all around the world.

Berkeley, 1964

In January 1964, Owsley presented himself at the front door of a run-down rooming house on Berkeley Way known as the Brown Shoe, where a room was for rent. Since everybody who lived there was already smoking grass and Owsley began talking about drugs as soon as he saw the room, the current occupants literally begged him to move in.

Charles Perry, who was living there while completing his studies in Middle Eastern languages at the University of California, Berkeley, before going on to write the dope column for *Rolling Stone* magazine under the pseudonym Smokestack El Ropo, had given the rooming house its name after seeing a cartoon drawn by a friend lampooning a popular radio commercial for Buster Brown shoes and because the house was "so very, very brown."

As Perry would later write of his first meeting with Owsley Stanley, "Forty-five minutes later, when he hadn't *stopped* talking about drugs, we weren't so sure he was cool. Not really tall, he had a sort of hulking manner anyhow and a wary look as if constantly planning an end run. . . . His conversation was like a series of lectures on the radar electronics he'd learned in the air force, the Russian grammar he'd studied when he was thinking of becoming a Russian Orthodox monk, the automotive technology he'd mastered while redesigning the engine of his MG."

When Owsley moved into his room, he brought with him "boxes full of stuff like ballet shoes, a complete bee keeper's outfit, and a painting in progress that showed the arm of Christ on the cross, portrayed more or less from Christ's point of view." As Perry soon learned, "the most amazing thing" about "this flagrant advocate for drugs" was that "he had only been smoking grass for a few weeks when he first moved in."

During the recent semester break, Owsley had driven down to Los Angeles. At "a funky little coffeehouse near LA City College," he ran into an old friend named Will Spires, who was going to Pasadena to score some pot. Owsley gave Spires a lift and then smoked marijuana for the first time in his life with Spires in Owsley's MG while it was parked on the side of the road. Promptly getting stoned, Owsley felt disoriented but thought the experience was interesting. He then got more and more into it over the next few weeks.

After he had returned to Berkeley, Owsley got hold of "a huge stash of Heavenly Blue morning glory seeds," which contained a chemical similar to lysergic acid. Although Owsley would later say that he never took any of them himself, he did put up three-by-five cards on virtually every bulletin board on campus advertising 250 morning glory seeds for sale for a dollar along with the address for a post office box. Eventually, he wound up trading all of the seeds for speed.

During his methedrine phase, Owsley began driving everyone in the rooming house crazy by running around all night long and then racing outside to ride his motorcycle at three thirty in the morning. Having already dropped out of the university after taking classes for two semesters, he was now working as a technician at KGO-TV in San Francisco. Not long after he had persuaded everyone at the rooming house to shoot speed with him, Owsley was evicted and moved to 1647 Virginia Street.

Searching for a scale to weigh some of the speed he had acquired in exchange for his morning glory seeds, Owsley walked into the chemistry lab in Latimer Hall at the University of California, Berkeley, on a gorgeous spring Friday afternoon. Clad in a black leather jacket, jeans, and leather boots, he went up to the only other person there, an attractive young woman with dark hair in a lab coat who was busily dismantling the glassware she had just used in a distillation experiment.

After she told him that the female student he was looking for had left an hour ago, he asked her why she was studying chemistry and how much she knew about psychedelics such as marijuana and morning glory seeds, which he considered an interesting field of research. Although she had already told him that she was engaged to a biologist, Owsley invited her to join him and his girlfriend for coffee at the Caffe Mediterraneum, the well-known Berkeley hangout on Telegraph Avenue where caffe latte may have been invented. After she had agreed to do so, he went off to use the Ainsworth electronic scales in the adjoining "clean" room.

Three days after she had sat down with Owsley and his girl-friend for coffee and baklava at Caffe Med, he had somehow pried "her away from her boyfriend who smoked a pipe and wore tweed suits with leather elbows, and she changed her mind about grad school."

Then twenty-two years old, Melissa Diane Cargill had grown up in the San Joaquin Valley, where her father had picked crops on various farms. The youngest of five children, she had been able to afford to attend the University of California, Berkeley, on loans designed to aid students who were interested in studying science. After her first year at the university, she had also begun working part-time to help support herself.

Before meeting Owsley in the lab at Latimer Hall, her career goal had been to become a research chemist in the life sciences. Charles Perry would later describe her as "a cute little honeybee with tender, intellectual eyes." She and Owsley were soon living together at what would in time come to be known as the Green Factory at 1647 Virginia Street.

There, Owsley got turned on to *Meet the Beatles!*, the first Beatles album released in America, and LSD. "I remember the first time I took acid, and I walked outside and the cars were kissing the parking meters. But that went away after a while." The first dose he ingested contained about one hundred milligrams of acid. He was then given a number four capsule with white powder inside that had been synthesized either by the Sandoz pharmaceutical company in Switzerland or in Czechoslovakia.

When Owsley's cousin came to visit him in Berkeley, the two of them split the capsule. "And I found out I had never taken real acid. God, if one person had taken that cap! It must have had five hundred micrograms in it. I swear to God. It was *potent!* Both my cousin and I went on quite a trip. And it was at the conclusion of that trip that I realized what real LSD was all about. And after that, I tried to get some more. I couldn't get any, so I thought, 'Well, shit, if I can't get any, obviously there's only one other way out. Go to the library.' All the organic synthetic chemistry that I know is about the stuff I picked up in a few weeks in the UC library."

While the myth has always been that Owsley learned how to synthesize LSD on his own, he was now living with a trained chemist who knew how to go about doing this, and who had also just taken acid with him for the first time. As Melissa Cargill would later say, "In the early days, I viewed LSD as a legal, interesting, organic chemistry synthesis. We wanted to produce a measured, reliable dose of high quality LSD. Tests on our results revealed a higher purity than Sandoz LSD."

The substance in question, LSD-25, the twenty-fifth derivative of lysergic acid diethylamide, had first been synthesized on November 16, 1938, by Dr. Albert Hofmann at the Sandoz laboratories in Basel, Switzerland, while he was trying to create a respiratory and circulatory stimulant. Five years later, on April 16, 1943, Hofmann accidentally ingested a small amount of the substance. Returning home, he lay down and "in a dream-like state, with eyes closed . . . perceived an uninterrupted stream of fantastic pictures, extraordinary shapes with intense, kaleidoscopic play of colors." After two hours, the condition faded away.

Three days later, on April 19, 1943, Hofmann intentionally ingested 250 micrograms of LSD. After beginning to experience intense shifts in perception, he asked his laboratory assistant to accompany him home. Because the use of automobiles in Switzerland was restricted during the war, they made the journey on bicycles. The anniversary of the first deliberate LSD trip ever taken continues to be celebrated by those enamored of the substance as Bicycle Day.

After a period of rampant paranoia and fear, Hofmann began to "enjoy the unprecedented colors and plays of shapes that persisted behind my closed eyes. Kaleidoscopic, fantastic images surged in on me, alternating, variegated, opening and then closing themselves in circles and spirals, exploding in colored fountains, rearranging and hybridizing themselves in constant flux." Based on his experiences with the drug, Hofmann became convinced that LSD could be used as a powerful psychiatric tool.

An odorless, colorless substance that in its pure form is mildly bitter, LSD can be derived from ergot, a grain fungus that typically grows on rye. Sensitive to oxygen, ultraviolet light, and chlorine, especially in solution, it can last for years if kept away from light and moisture at low temperature. Dissolving LSD in tap water can completely eliminate the substance because of the chlorine in the water. The well-known biochemist and psychopharmacologist Sasha Shulgin called it "an unusually fragile molecule."

As both Owsley and Melissa Cargill soon learned, manufacturing LSD required not only a vast array of laboratory equipment but also far more experience in the field of organic chemistry than either of them had at the time. Which did not stop Owsley from plunging headfirst into the process. After having installed a heavy-duty ventilation fan in the bathroom at 1647 Virginia Street, he set up a makeshift lab and went to work.

Somehow, the police got wind that methedrine was being sold to teenagers at this location. On February 21, 1965, a squad of state drug cops based in San Francisco raided the house and confiscated what they thought was speed. "They took one box of various assorted labeled and unlabeled chemicals. None of it was unfinished methedrine. Among the chemicals was an unmarked sample of dimethyl amphetamine which I had made and was playing around with but it was both physically and mentally inert. It was not legally a drug, just a chemical."

Not at all cowed by the charges he was now facing, Owsley promptly hired Arthur Harris, who was then the vice mayor of Berkeley, to represent him in court. Confounding all notions of what a speed dealer was supposed to look like, Owsley "showed up at one hearing in denim trousers and jacket; at the next hearing, he wore a sharp Italian suit. He broadcast dangerous, edgy resentment rather than decent fear. He managed to beat the charges anyway."

The way that Owsley always liked to tell the story, the bust on Virginia Street was just yet another example of how he could never be deterred by those who knew less than him. "In the charges that were filed against me, the lab analysis said the di-meth sample was speed. I thought they were simply lying as there was no way the official police lab could have been that incompetent. We had to force them in court to furnish us with a sample to submit to an independent laboratory for analysis which proved them wrong, leading to dismissal of all charges."

The means by which Owsley had obtained enough money to hire a high-powered attorney, not to mention to also purchase the sharp Italian suit in which he appeared in court, was in fact by having sold methedrine. As Charles Perry would later note, "At the time of his Virginia Street bust, Owsley was not yet rich but he had already made a decent amount of money by dealing from the sample of methedrine that a chemical supply house had provided him for his fictitious 'research on the effect of methedrine on the cortisone metabolism of rats.'

"It was a substantial sample, about a pound or so, and I got the impression they had provided it to him free with the understanding that if his 'study' got funded, he'd go to them for all his subsequent needs. In effect, the company was subsidizing Owsley's first grop- ing efforts in chemical synthesis by allowing him to deal lab quality meth to grateful Bay Area speeders."

Owsley had obtained the sample by requesting it on stationery that he had printed up for the entirely fictitious Bear Research Group. On the off chance that the chemical company might sud- denly decide to inspect his research facility, Owsley had then tried to inveigle Perry, who had just taken a job tending rats in one of the University of California Psychology Department animal labs, to be- come part of his scheme." He wanted me to bring a dozen rat cages over to his place," Perry would later write, "and stand around in my white lab coat.

"Frankly, I hoped he'd never test our palship by calling on that favor. I didn't want anything to do with his current scene, which consisted of hanging around with some truly sordid speed freaks, such as a guy who'd stand around all evening jerkily leafing through nudist magazines—front to back, back to front, front to back again— muttering, 'Process. It's all *process*,' while the other speed freaks in the room argued about who was alerting the police they imagined to be watching their every move by casting a shadow on the win- dow shade."

On the night that the Green Factory on Virginia Street was raided, one of Owsley's friends walked by the house and then alerted

Perry that it might have been busted. Perry then called the police to ask if another friend who had been minding the house for Owsley had been arrested. After being informed that the friend was now in jail, Perry quickly got in touch with Melissa, "who reflected for about a minute and a half before pouring a pound or so of methedrine down a Berkeley storm drain with the cheerful resignation she could always summon in a pinch."

Secure in the knowledge that all the incriminating evidence concerning what he had actually been doing at the Green Factory had now neatly been disposed of, Owsley presented his case with impunity in court and walked away completely unscathed from this particular brush with the law.

Unwilling to quit when he was ahead, Owsley then presented himself "at the property lockup to regain my lab gear. I was stonewalled. The leading officer of the drug squad refused to release my property, telling me to 'Go get a court order.' They had never had anyone ask for a return of evidence before. I assume that all those who managed to beat their cases had just abandoned the gear.

"My opinion was that the act of abandoning my claim was the equivalent of admitting that I was really guilty and they had just missed the evidence. In a few days, my lawyer obtained a court order naming the drug agency and the officer in charge by name. The cops were clearly wrong by retaining my property as evidence once the case had been dismissed and the court agreed."

Returning to the police station, Owsley again demanded that he be given back his property. "'Where is your court order?' the smug bastard asked. I laid it on the counter and got a great rush from seeing his face as he read it. It was a really stupid career move on his part to engage me like that because it brought disgrace on the

police and they pinned it on him by name. After that, I never had
any further trouble from the drug squad."

What Owsley did not also tell the officer at the time was that
during the raid, the drug cops had "overlooked the residue of my
initial, unsuccessful attempt to cook acid as well as a bottle of waste
water containing traces of real methamphetamine base left over
from a steam distillation I had undertaken months before and forgotten about in the clutter, which had also hid it from the cops."

Unable to retrieve the books she needed to study for her courses
at the university from the house on Virginia Street because of the
bust, Melissa Cargill withdrew from school. "To be honest," she
would later say, "my studies had suffered and become less meaning-
ful as Owsley, drugs, and music became more interesting."

Intent on continuing to pursue what so far had been their fairly
unsuccessful attempts to synthesize LSD, the two of them left Berkeley and headed for Los Angeles. Using his Bear Research Group
stationery, Owsley then began buying large amounts of the raw
material he would need to make the purest acid ever to hit the
streets in America.

5

Making Acid

❦

Setting up shop in a rented two-bedroom house at 2205 Lafler Road in Los Angeles not far from the campus of Cal State LA, Owsley ordered one hundred grams of lysergic monohydrate from the Cyclo Chemical Corporation as well as another forty grams from the International Chemical and Nuclear Corporation (ICN). Along with each request, Owsley also submitted a signed affidavit stating he would use the material for research purposes only.

The first hundred-gram bottle of lysergic monohydrate, for which Owsley paid $4,000 in $100 bills by drawing upon his apparently endless cash reserve from the sale of methedrine in Berkeley, arrived on March 30, 1965. The substance he was sent by ICN, which had been founded and was then being run by the aptly named Milan Panic, who would later serve as the prime minister of Yugoslavia, was "a nasty brown powder" that Owsley promptly returned after discovering that it was of no use to him at all in making LSD.

By May, Owsley and Melissa had successfully synthesized their first batch of LSD, which Owsley then began distributing by taking orders for it by mail at a Sunset Boulevard address. As word on the street began spreading about the incredible power and purity of his product, Owsley used the proceeds from the sales to buy three more hundred-gram bottles of lysergic monohydrate from the Cyclo Chemical Corporation, thereby bringing his total investment in the project to $16,000, the equivalent of about $120,000 today.

Despite how impressive his work in the laboratory had been, Owsley would insist to the end of his days that he was never a chemist. "There's no more chemistry to making LSD than to baking a bloody cake. You just have to know how to do it. What parts to use, what temperature to set the oven. . . . Most of it is published, and that which isn't published is available to an investigative mind. The correct and accepted term for those who make the entheogens is cook—I like to think of it as sort of gourmet chef, master of fine mental cuisine."

By now, Owsley had also already immersed himself in *The Kybalion: Hermetic Philosophy*, a book he had found in the Shambhala bookstore in Berkeley in the fall of 1964. Originally published in 1908, *The Kybalion* was an exploration and explanation of alchemy that had most likely been written by Paul Foster Case, Michael Whitty, and William Walker Atkinson, who had chosen to call themselves the Three Initiates.

Although the Free Speech Movement on the campus of the University of California in Berkeley, which would spawn similar protests at other institutions of higher learning all across America in years to come, was then at its peak, Owsley was already marching to the beat of a very different drummer. Completely ignoring the continuing series of student demonstrations that eventually resulted in a mass arrest as "a college kid thing," Owsley plunged so deeply into *The Kybalion* that it soon became the guide he used to steer through every aspect of his life.

"If you were not ready, the book was absolutely meaningless. It either meant everything to you or it meant nothing because it said the lips of wisdom were closed except to the ear of understanding. For me, it was the key to alchemy and to understanding what the universe was all about because it put all the things I then experienced on acid into total context.

"Alchemy was mental transformation. It was never about transforming substances. Those were all allegories. The lead and the gold is the lead of the primitive nature into the gold of the enlightened man. It was always about that. Alchemy didn't begin talking about turning lead into gold until it had to deal with the Church during the early Middle Ages."

The widely used occult phrase "as above, so below" soon became the foundation of Owsley's belief that whatever happened on any physical, emotional, or mental level while he was tripping was not a fantasy. "I'd take a bit of acid, and Melissa would say, 'No, this is real. You've got to deal with it.' 'Oh, okay. It's not the drug. It must be something I didn't know about.' Once I accepted something that I wouldn't have received normally as being real, different things happened, and that was the key to it all."

Owsley also soon came to believe that his state of mind while he was making acid would affect the result. "LSD is something that goes from being absolutely inert to so powerful that twenty-five micrograms will cause a change in your consciousness. You're concentrating a lot of mental energy on one package. And if you believe, as I did, that the universe is a mental thing, a creation in the mind of a being that is actually creating time and space, then everything is mental. So when I had something that would affect the minds of thousands and thousands of people in the palm of my hand, how could I not believe that?"

While it has been widely reported that Owsley and Melissa came up with 1.5 million doses of LSD during their time in LA, he would later dispute this claim. "I never, ever estimated how many doses the stash might make as I had no idea what my real yield might be. The potential might have been about a little more than 1.2 million doses but we only got out about 800,000 in all formats, of which about half were given away for free." At an average price of $3 a dose, it was still a huge amount of money, some of which Owsley liked to carry around with him in $100 bills that he kept in his boots.

Still pretty much a rank amateur at the difficult business of synthesizing LSD, Owsley used sulfur trioxide as the reagent. The highly corrosive chemical could also cause serious burns if it was inhaled or ingested while being handled. The material was also "difficult to get rid of," and Owsley would later remember "dropping some off a bridge one time and watching it combine with the moisture in the air to form a huge cloud of sulfuric acid."

The LSD he was now making had side effects as well. "When you start to work with it, you absorb it and you get high. You have to back off for a day, and the next day you get more of it and it doesn't do anything. And by about the third or fourth day, you could probably drink a gram of it and nothing would happen. But it does space you out, and you get further and further from reality as the weeks go on. I found out that about three weeks was all I could handle. At a time."

The immediate widespread popularity of the LSD that Owsley was now producing in bulk soon made him realize he was embarking on a journey that few people had ever before undertaken. "I started doing this acid thing, and the first thing that I sat down and thought about was—'You know, a lot of people are in jail because of doing this. This is very dangerous. This is like venturing into a battlefield with a lot of guns you have never even looked at.' I had no idea what I had to do to protect myself or how to negotiate. I had no idea who was good and who wasn't.

"And so I had to focus all of my incredible concentration on figuring this out as fast as possible. I developed ways of talking to people while watching their expressions and listening to their answers while formulating the next thing I would say based on what they had said, and then watching the way in which they reacted to that. I had spent a year in acting training, and that helped me learn how to do this."

Although it was not his preferred method of doing business, Owsley would sometimes sell LSD directly to people whom he trusted, who would then go off and resell the acid on their own. "I never fronted anything to anyone since I felt that fronting dope made the two people 'partners' whereas exchanging money for the material was just a straightforward business transaction between independent operators."

While he was in Los Angeles, Owsley sold some of his newly made LSD to a talented Berkeley-based folk guitarist named Perry Lederman, who then "told people I had made it, and that was how my name got attached to it. I said, 'Oh, fuck, Perry, why did you do that?' And he said, 'Oh, I don't know.' I had nothing to do with that and I did everything I could to stay out of it. I wouldn't even let people take pictures of me. I wasn't trying to create a fucking myth—I was just trying to stay out of jail."

What neither Owsley nor Melissa knew at the time was that Captain Alfred Tremblay, the commander of the Los Angeles narcotics division, had already begun regularly emptying the garbage cans outside their house on Lafler Road. A year later, when he appeared before a Senate subcommittee in Washington, DC, Tremblay testified that he knew LSD had been manufactured and distributed from that address. Tremblay also displayed several order forms he had retrieved from Owsley's garbage, including one from Portland, Oregon, with a request for forty capsules and the postscript "love to Melissa."

By the time Owsley and Melissa returned to Berkeley in April 1965, he had, in Charles Perry's words, "become a rather vocal disparager of methedrine." Nonetheless, Charles Perry later recalled that Owsley showed up at one of the "little ostentatiously informal gatherings" at which "Bay Area psychedelic chemists" liked to show off "their accomplishments. From the way Owsley talked about them, I gathered there was some spirit of sharing, some simple enthusiasm, and a certain tincture of competitiveness.

"Owsley proudly produced methedrine (or maybe some other amphetamine) which he had synthesized not from chemical precursors but from the ephedra plant. I don't know where he got it but a number of species grow wild and I believe Ephedra funerea (Mormon tea) was actually available in health food and herbalist stores. So it was organic meth. He would have done this purely for the pleasure of the accomplishment because by that time he had come to oppose amphetamines as a high."

In a gesture of friendship during this same period, Owsley

handed Perry a capsule of his newly minted LSD. Forty minutes after ingesting it, Perry was "two-dimensional, fading into the Wall of the World Womb, which turned into the wall of an Egyptian tomb, and I was a painting of an ancient Egyptian on a tomb wall with hieroglyphics sprouting from my elbows and knees and disappearing down the wall too fast for my two-dimensional eyes ever to read."

Panicked, Perry walked a mile and a half to find a girl from the rooming house so she could help talk him down from his trip. When Perry told Owsley the next day that the LSD had turned him into a painting, he said, "Oh, that's right. . . . You had one of those first ones. Hey, they were too heavy. You should have only taken half."

Many years later, Grateful Dead lyricist and Electronic Frontier Foundation cofounder John Perry Barlow attended a conference where he met Albert Hofmann. When Barlow told Hofmann of his connection with the Grateful Dead, the Swiss chemist asked him if he knew this Owsley fellow.

After Barlow said that he did, Hofmann told him that although he had seen quite a lot of formations of LSD, he was quite impressed with what Owsley had done as he was the only one who had ever got the crystallization process correct. On every level, it was the ultimate confirmation that Owsley had come up with the real thing.

6

Pranksters and Angels

❧

In what would eventually come to be recognized as an iconic evening in the formation of the counterculture in America, the Hells Angels turned up in force on August 7, 1965, to party with Ken Kesey and the Merry Pranksters at Kesey's sprawling wood-frame house in La Honda. Hunter Thompson, who had already written about the motorcycle gang for *The Nation* magazine and was then researching his forthcoming book about them, was there. So too were Richard Alpert and Allen Ginsberg, who would later write a short, elegiac poem about the event.

Based in large part on a fifteen-page report that had been issued in March by the California attorney general as well as extensive coverage in mass-circulation magazines such as *Newsweek, Life,* and *Time,* the Hells Angels had already achieved an astonishing level of nationwide notoriety as a terrifying band of outlaws who only loved their motorcycles and were always ready to wreak havoc at a moment's notice on anyone who got in their way.

Because of Kesey's utter fearlessness and incredible personal charisma, as well as the huge amount of beer and LSD that the Pranksters had laid on for the event, the wildly out-of-control party, which included a gang bang that both Hunter Thompson and Tom Wolfe later described in great detail, was a roaring success. The event was also seen as proof that acid was so powerful an elixir that it could transform even the most fearsome band of outlaws imaginable into relatively peaceful human beings.

In truth, the Merry Pranksters and the Hells Angels had almost nothing in common. Despite how crazy the Pranksters could sometimes get while tripping, they were for the most part well-educated dropouts who saw themselves as part of a significant social experiment. Five years before Tom Wolfe would coin the term, their odd alliance with the Hells Angels was an early form of radical chic.

While it may now be difficult to understand why a band of psychedelic loonies would want to reach out to an outlaw motorcycle gang for any reason whatsoever, it should be remembered that much of what went on during the 1960s was motivated by an unceasing quest for authenticity. Whatever else anyone might have had to say about the Hells Angels, they were definitely real, often in the most terrifying way imaginable.

Despite the widely held belief that LSD could transform lions into lambs, nine weeks after the Hells Angels had taken acid at Kesey's party, they violently attacked a large group of marchers in Oakland led by Allen Ginsberg who were peacefully protesting against the war in Vietnam. As they mauled the demonstrators, the Angels shouted, "Go back to Russia, you fucking Communists!"

Safely ensconced in the LSD scene in Berkeley that he was largely responsible for having created, Owsley had for months been resisting the efforts of a black friend named Gaylord to accompany him down to La Honda to visit Kesey. Based on all that Owsley knew about the Hells Angels, he considered them "to be the most violent guys I'd ever heard about. The thought of going down there and hanging out with them didn't sound like it was going to be safe, and certainly not fun."

After hopping into Gaylord's car one day in October 1965, Owsley finally made the fifty-five-mile journey that would irrevocably alter his life. Then thirty years old, the same age as Owsley, Kesey was a powerfully built man who had been a champion wrestler in high school and then at the University of Oregon. Having already achieved national fame by writing *One Flew Over the Cuckoo's Nest* and *Sometimes a Great Notion*, Kesey had also recently been busted for possession of marijuana. While all this might have intimidated someone who was meeting him for the first time, that person would not have been Owsley.

Sidling right up to Kesey, he introduced himself by saying, "I'm Owsley." Having never heard the name before, Kesey just stared at him as if to say, "Okay. Fine. You're Owsley. So?" After a few moments of awkward silence, Owsley handed Kesey several hits of LSD. "Before I got there, some guy named John the Chemist had been making their acid. When I met him, Kesey already had a good supply and so was not very interested in what I had, suspicion being one of his strong suits."

Despite this lukewarm initial reception, Owsley found the scene interesting and returned to the house on La Honda Road several times. With him, he brought more of the product that Kesey and

his fellow Pranksters had already learned was far superior to the
LSD they had been taking.

For Owsley, hanging out with Kesey "was sort of like getting
strapped to a rocket sled. The stuff that those guys would do with
your head, and the drugs and everything else, was nothing like
anything else I had experienced before. It was absolutely dramatic.
And it *was* true. The Angels turned out to be some of the farthest-
out people in my life I had ever met. They were just cut free by this
thing. It was like a key."

Involved for the first time with someone whose personality ri-
valed or exceeded his own, Owsley soon realized that Kesey "was
the kind of guy that reached out, took your knobs, and tweaked them
all the way to ten. All of them. And the whole scene was running at
ten all the time. It was almost as sudden, and as different, as discovering psychedelics themselves for the first time, at another level."

Not surprisingly, Owsley never bonded with Kesey or the Pranksters, whom he considered to be "a bunch of people who were goofing off and getting high on acid once a week and playing around
with what it did to their heads. There was a lot of pretension, and it
was almost impossible to get Kesey to listen to anybody else and understand or accept what they had to say. You just couldn't give him
any kind of advice or anything. It was always all about Kesey." With
the possible exception of his father, Owsley had finally come into
contact with someone he could not control.

Another issue on which Owsley and Kesey differed was how
much LSD it was cool to take at one time. "Two hundred and fifty
micrograms was a pretty strong dose, but I thought it was the right
one because that was what Albert Hofmann had taken before going
off on his bicycle ride. When you get to four hundred micrograms,

I don't care who you are, you just totally lose it. Kesey liked to take four hundred. He wanted to lose it."

Unlikely as it would have seemed to Owsley before he made his way down to Kesey's house in La Honda for the first time, the only person in the Prankster scene with whom he formed a lasting relationship was John Terrance Tracy, better known to his fellow Hells Angels as Terry the Tramp.

Standing six feet two inches tall and weighing 210 pounds, Terry the Tramp looked, in Hunter Thompson's words, like "a cross between Joe Palooka and the Wandering Jew." He had "massive arms, a full beard, shoulder-length black hair and a wild, jabbering demeanor." Twenty-eight years old when Owsley met him, Terry the Tramp had by then already been arrested for battery, rape, petty theft, and public cunnilingus without ever having been convicted of a felony.

One of the four Hells Angels who had been arrested in Seaside, California, in September 1964 for allegedly raping two teenaged girls, an incident that made headline news before all of the charges were eventually thrown out of court, Terry the Tramp had also lived in Hollywood, where he had acquired an Actors' Equity card.

On the night of the fabled Hells Angels party at Kesey's house, Terry the Tramp had seized a microphone and told the cops parked across the road that while they were out there keeping watch, they should be thinking "about that little old *wife* of yours back home with some dirty old Hell's Angel crawlin' up *between her thighs*!" Asking "the worthless fuzz" if they were hungry, he then offered to bring them all some chili if there was any left over, but counseled them not to rush home so their wives could enjoy themselves to the fullest.

The way Owsley saw it, "Terry the Tramp was a very cosmic dude. He was a lovely fellow and one of the most amazing people I knew from that era. He once told me, 'Whoo, I love to get into a fight on acid!' I said, 'Why?' 'Because the other guy is in slow motion.' He also told me that if you ever got into a fight, the first blow counts for ten."

Being accepted by the Hells Angels was a massive boost to Owsley's already outsized ego. "There I was, very nonviolent, and I was with all these Hells Angels who liked to punch each other out for the fun of it. I'd get around them half-stoned and I'd have the feeling they were like minor devils in the presence of the chief. I got this feeling of awe and respect from all these very powerful, intelligent, dangerous beings, and I could not believe I had really earned it."

Brilliantly, Owsley viewed the Hells Angels' relationship with cops as being much like "wolves were to dogs. They both wore uniforms and were highly organized and very dangerous and armed. But the cops were a little more under control, like dogs. The Angels were the wolves. But they were the same kind and that was why they had this dance going on."

Based in great part on the very pure acid Owsley was supplying them for their own use that they were also then reselling on the street, the Hells Angels soon became a weird but integral part of the counterculture. The consequences of this unholy union would eventually prove tragic not only for the culture itself but also for Terry the Tramp.

Not until Owsley heard Jerry Garcia play for the first time before Owsley's legendary freakout at the Muir Beach Acid Test did he realize he was "a lot more like the Dead" than the Pranksters and decide "to go to work for the most amazing group ever and have a fabulous time of it. The Dead were going to go there anyway. I just hitched a ride and tried to make a positive contribution."

7

Trips Festival

On many levels, the psychedelic sixties truly began at the Trips Festival held at Longshoremen's Hall at 400 North Point Street in San Francisco on the weekend of January 21, 22, and 23, 1966. Stewart Brand, who would go on to create the *Whole Earth Catalog*, came up with the original concept along with a musician and visual artist named Ramon Sender. With Ken Kesey and the Merry Pranksters as the featured attraction, by far the wildest of the three events took place on Saturday night.

Kesey, who had just been given a six-month sentence on a work farm as well as six months of probation for his marijuana bust at La Honda, had made front-page news in San Francisco just two days earlier by getting arrested yet again along with his companion Carolyn Adams, aka Mountain Girl, for smoking a joint on the roof of Brand's apartment in North Beach.

No doubt in part to show their continuing support for Kesey, somewhere between three thousand and five thousand revelers who were stoned out of their heads on LSD that Owsley had provided jammed a hall that was only supposed to hold seventeen hundred people. In the words of Grateful Dead biographer Dennis McNally, "There were simply more people tripping in a single room . . . than anyone had ever seen before."

As Jerry Garcia would later say, "It was total insanity. I mean total, wall-to-wall, gonzo lunacy. . . . Everybody was just partying furiously. There were people jumping off balconies onto blankets and then bouncing up and down. I mean, there was *incredible* shit going on. Plus, it was like old home week. I met and saw everybody I had ever known. Every beatnik, every hippie, every coffeehouse hangout person from all over the state was there, all freshly psychedelicized."

What with Hells Angels punching out members of other motorcycle clubs in the hallways as one of the Pranksters tried to force Big Brother and the Holding Company off the stage after they had performed just one song, the scene was so crazy that no one could control it. Which did not stop Bill Graham, who had only just begun putting on shows at the Fillmore Auditorium and had been brought in to help run the event, from doing all he could to stop the Pranksters from letting people in for free.

After running all over the hall with a clipboard in his hand in search of Kesey, Graham finally found him standing at the back door letting in a constant stream of bikers. To keep the law from knowing he was there, Kesey was attending the event in a silver space suit with a helmet. After trying in vain to get Kesey's attention, Graham finally lost control and began screaming at him. Without saying a word, Kesey simply flipped the visor of his helmet down and went right on doing as he pleased.

As Bob Weir of the Grateful Dead would later say of Bill Graham that night, "We were with the Pranksters and the buzz was, 'Who's that asshole with the clipboard?'" Aside from Jerry Garcia, with whom Graham would forge a lifelong bond on Sunday night by trying to put Garcia's shattered guitar back together so the Dead could play (which they never did), the only other person at the Trips Festival who understood what Bill Graham was all about was Owsley.

"It was completely out of control and he was trying to control it, and of course he couldn't, because the harder you tried to grab it, the more slippery it became. I was real stoned when I came into contact with Bill, and I could see right through all the bullshit, and I realized he was half-terrified by what it was and was doing everything he could to control it and to suppress the realization that there was something special going on there besides something that was obviously making money."

Owsley brought Tim Scully with him to the Trips Festival. Then twenty-six years old, Scully had skipped his senior year in high school to begin attending the University of California at Berkeley, where he majored in mathematical physics. Having already built a small computer in middle school and a liner accelerator in high school, Scully had left the university in 1964 to work as an electronic design consultant.

A few hours after having mailed in his tax return on April 15, 1965, Scully had taken LSD for the first time. Possessed by the notion that acid was a better solution to society's problems than technology, Scully then spent months tracking "down the source of his dose," who was of course Owsley. After spending weeks carefully checking Scully out, Owsley brought him to the Trips Festival to see how he would react, and the two then began working together on assembling state-of-the-art sound equipment for the Dead as well as the wholesale manufacture of high-quality LSD.

One week after the Trips Festival, on January 29, 1966, Owsley joined the Grateful Dead at the Sound City Acid Test. During the event, held in a radio station in San Francisco, the band tried to record what they had been doing live to accompany the swirling madness created by the Pranksters. During the evening, Bob Weir "first sort of logged into Owsley. He was dressed in medieval garb, had a pageboy haircut, and was wearing a ruffled shirt, and he was a dandy. Of course I was loaded on LSD, so all that had its own little resonance with me.

"I was on Owsley acid when I met Owsley, and he seemed like one of us. I was eighteen years old and he was as old as Kesey, at least thirty, but they were both more like kids than most kids you were going to see. We connected right away because he was a very, very interesting guy and seemed to know something about everything, and that appealed to me.

"If you got involved in a discussion with Owsley even back then, you kind of had to pack a lunch. I think Phil was his closest contact in the band. They had already bonded because they both had really high IQs and real good retention of information and they were both really curious. Together, they added up to different kaleidoscopes, if you will."

Then twenty-five years old, Phil Lesh had attended Berkeley High School and the College of San Mateo before transferring to the University of California in Berkeley, where he dropped out after a single semester. Originally a violin player, he had also studied the trumpet and was an avid devotee of avant-garde classical music and free jazz. While working as an unpaid recording engineer at KPFA, Lesh had met Jerry Garcia, who talked him into becoming the bass player for the band that was then still known as the Warlocks. Unlike Garcia, Lesh had been formally trained and so could read music as well as write charts.

Lesh and Owsley had first connected with each other at the Fillmore Acid Test on January 8, 1966. Having last seen a completely freaked-out Owsley dragging a chair across the floor in Muir Beach, Lesh thought Owsley now looked "like a conquering hero or some Robin Hood figure out of swashbuckling antiquity." Wearing "an Aussie digger hat and a leather cape," Owsley seemed to Lesh "every inch the figure of the psychedelic warrior . . . a man who knows he's on to something cosmic and eternal."

Walking up to Owsley, Lesh extended his hand and said, "So, you're Owsley. I feel as if I've known you through many lifetimes." Immediately taking the conversation to another level, Owsley replied, "You have, and you will through many more to come." Lesh then felt as though he were living in Owsley's head, which may have been "the result of all the trips I'd taken using his product."

Never one to pass on an opportunity, Owsley then asked what he could do for the band. "Phil said they did not have a manager. Having no interest in that role at all, I declined the offer. He then said they had no sound man, and I figured I could be good at that since I had audio experience in radio and TV. By the time of the Trips Festival, I *was* their sound man."

At the Sound City Acid Test, Owsley and Lesh spent a good deal of time together raving at one another. "Other than Jerry," Lesh would later write, "I'd not known anyone with as great a breadth of interests before, and it seemed to me that he was actually articulating some of the fuzzy visions we'd had regarding the Meaning Of It All." For Lesh, hanging out with Owsley was "like being in a science fiction novel."

Right from the start of what became their enduring friendship, Owsley felt much the same way about Lesh. "Phil was the one I met first, and whenever we would get high together, we would hook up telepathically. It's funny because in many ways we were absolutely opposite. He's a Pisces born in the year of the dragon and I'm a Capricorn born in the year of the dog, but I had grown up with my father, who was also born in the year of the dragon and so I could always tell when I was pushing too hard with Phil in the wrong direction and when to back off."

Although Owsley did not know anyone who had any real experience managing a rock band, he then met Rock Scully. By then, Scully had already helped the Family Dog collective put on a show featuring the Lovin' Spoonful at Longshoreman's Hall on October 24, 1965. In Scully's words, "He said, 'I've been watching you, Scully, and you're doing a good job. He really wanted to talk business and then he said, 'You've got to hear this band.' They were still the Warlocks then, and although I had already heard about them from Kesey, I had forgotten about them pretty quickly."

Then twenty-four years old, Scully had grown up in Carmel, California. His stepfather, Milton Mayer, was a well-known Quaker activist who had once hosted his own network radio show. After graduating from Earlham College in Indiana, Scully had attended

San Francisco State, where he became involved in a series of massive civil rights demonstrations. During the summer of 1965, Scully had begun managing the Charlatans, a psychedelic band who were doing an extended residency at the Red Dog Saloon in Virginia City, Nevada.

Scully finally saw the Grateful Dead perform for the first time at the Fillmore Acid Test on January 8, 1966. Although he told Owsley that the Dead were "extraordinarily ugly and would probably never make it commercially," Scully also confessed that he had "never heard a more amazing band musically."

Owsley knew that "the Dead needed a manager and Rock had been involved in the Family Dog stuff. None of my other friends knew anything about managing or had any experience doing this. So it was a matter of nobody knowing how to do anything and the musicians being exploited by most managers while having no say in what they did. I shared that with Jerry Garcia and the Dead, and they all thought it was good idea for me to talk to Rock about this. So I suggested it to him."

Having set on his sights on Rock Scully as the person who was best suited to manage the Grateful Dead, Owsley pursued him in what had by now become his usual manner by getting Scully higher than he had ever before been. "Owsley saw me as a businessman who was interested in music. I told him where I lived and said we could talk about me managing the Dead. So he came over to my house in the upper Haight and brought some DMT and said, 'You gotta smoke this before we talk about anything.' We did, and instantly it was as complete an enveloping hallucination as you can possibly achieve on anything. Almost like an elevator. A friend of mine was there and he took one puff and fell over."

Before they smoked DMT together, Owsley had asked Scully to go through his extensive record collection and play some music. "So I put on the first Rolling Stones album and it really helped. It was a shred of reality I could hold on to while I was sitting on this rug and then swimming in it, and everything I saw looked like that. Early on, Kesey had told me, 'If you're ever tripping and you go down that hallway and open the wrong door, just remember it was something you took. Don't get afraid because that will only make it worse. Just remember you took something and it'll wear off.' Which helped me save my ass."

When Scully finally came back down from the DMT about thirty minutes later, "Owsley was expounding on this theory about music and how it reverberated and vibrated with our nervous systems, and then he went on this whole ethno-musicology rap, which made absolute sense to me because I had studied the subject myself.

"He was talking about the importance of what I had been doing, and I hadn't really seen it before in that scope. He said, 'In the promoter position, you have to try to get the artist for as little as possible so you can make money. What I'm proposing to you now is that you protect the art and protect the musicians by becoming the manager of the Grateful Dead and trying to get as much money as you can for them.' He imprinted me with this, and I also think he thought he would have influence over me, which he did. He selected me and he selected Garcia as well because he saw that Kesey was getting too wild and was not going to focus on the band."

Once Scully and his partner, Danny Rifkin, had decided to throw their lot in with the Grateful Dead, Owsley continued to influence the musical direction in which the band was going by convening group sessions in his cottage in Berkeley. Long before the term *gearhead* had ever been invented, Owsley was already obsessive about procuring the best possible equipment for whatever task he was involved in at the moment.

Before ever meeting the Grateful Dead, Owsley had already purchased and installed a sound system in his thirty-five-by-fifty-five-foot living room in Berkeley that far surpassed what even the most fanatical hi-fi enthusiast at the time might have dreamed of owning. Looking like "something that someone had rescued from behind the screen at the local movie theater," his Altec Lansing Voice of the Theatre system consisted of two large wooden cabinets, each of which was "about the size of a small fridge." Equipped with a fifteen-inch speaker, a driver that was "about four inches in diameter," and "a little horn mounted on top," each cabinet weighed a hundred pounds. Owsley then ran the sound through a McIntosh amplifier with "two channels, forty watts per channel."

In Rock Scully's words, "Owsley brought us together in a whole other way because he had a cottage in Berkeley where there were no neighbors who could complain about the noise and the place was packed full of gear. He had tape decks and really good microphones and great speakers. It was the ideal haven that was just as high-tech in fidelity terms as you could get back then. He also had these tape loops, and so for Phil and Jerry and all of us, it was just a playground where we could get something going on a tape, start a loop, and then improvise on top of that."

When the Grateful Dead decided to follow the Pranksters to Los Angeles in February 1966 to play a series of Acid Tests down there,

Owsley provided the money that enabled them all to make the trip. The band departed so abruptly from San Francisco that Jerry Garcia left his yellow, four-door Corvair parked in a gas station in Palo Alto. All of Bob Weir's clothes were in the trunk, but neither he nor Garcia ever saw the car again.

After getting on a jet plane for the first time in his life, Phil Lesh flew to Los Angeles alongside Owsley. "It was a red-eye flight," Lesh would later write, "and we were the only two people in the back of a 707." Because Owsley was footing the bill, Melissa Cargill, Tim Scully, and Rock Scully (who were not related to each other), Danny Rifkin, and a friend of theirs named Ron Rakow also accompanied the band to LA.

Due in no small part to the high-quality LSD that Owsley was handing out at no cost to his new circle of musician friends, as well as his continuing willingness to bankroll the band with money he had made from the sale of his product on the streets throughout the Bay Area, the scene around the Grateful Dead had now started to expand at what would soon become an exponential rate.

8

LA Fadeaway

~⚬~

Thanks to the Pranksters, Owsley and the Grateful Dead came to ground in Los Angeles in a three-story pink stucco house on a street near West Adams Boulevard, not far from the Santa Monica Freeway in the Watts section of the city. As everyone soon discovered, their next-door neighbors did not take kindly to their arrival.

"We were living next to a black whorehouse," Owsley would later say. "The whores hated our loud music and would complain that it was driving off their johns. They used to throw pot seeds out of the window, and we found little pot plants growing between the two houses that weren't ours because we were careful about that. We thought the whorehouse was going to get us busted, but we brought the cops down on ourselves a few times because of the volume of the music that the Dead were playing."

Although Owsley quickly installed himself on the top floor and paid the rent while also providing food for all those in the house, he was not initially pleased by the move. "It wasn't my idea to go to LA. I was against it because I didn't see any point in it. The Dead were following the Acid Tests, and that turned out not to be a great idea, but it was more important to them than anything else. At regular shows in the Bay Area, they had been getting paid a hundred and twenty-five dollars, but they got nothing for playing an Acid Test. After I thought about it for a while, I realized we could do some shows ourselves down there and the band could practice a lot."

Along with Tim Scully, Owsley began modifying the sound of the band's guitars by installing a transformer that was connected to low-impedance cables to clean up the signal. Owsley and Tim Scully then built a stereo mixing panel and acquired an oscilloscope so they could check on the amplifiers during a show. After providing the Dead with expensive Sennheiser microphones, Owsley began obsessively recording all their performances so the band could hear how they had sounded onstage.

While all these innovations were significant advances in what was then still the primitive state of rock 'n' roll sound, the system Owsley had brought with him from his cottage in Berkeley soon proved to be less than ideally suited for use on the road. In Rock Scully's words, "The Voice of the Theatre speaker boxes were huge. Four of them would just about take up an office, but they were also alarmingly delicate and would constantly blow fuses and burn out so we had to haul spares along with them. We couldn't trust any promoter to provide us with enough electricity or clean electricity, so we also had these huge, incredibly heavy transformers that were just monsters and needed sledding."

What came to be known as "the lead sled" also took an incredibly

long time for Owsley and Tim Scully to set up onstage. The problem was compounded by Owsley's refusal to ever rush when he was
doing this. That everyone was also usually high on acid while the work
was going on only made it all seem to take just that much longer.

As Owsley and Scully were crouched over together onstage one
night soldering a transformer box onto Phil Lesh's amplifier, the
bass player began fantasizing about giving them both a swift kick
in the ass. Instead, all Lesh could do was just stand there and wait
for them to finish because he knew "this is the way it's going to be."

What regularly occurred onstage before the Grateful Dead performed in Los Angeles was nothing compared to what passed for
their daily life together. The communal-living scene inside the pink
stucco house in Watts was so utterly chaotic that horror stories about
it would be told over and over in the years to come. By far the most
colorful description appears in *Living with the Dead: Twenty Years on
the Bus with Garcia and the Grateful Dead*, Rock Scully's memoir of his
time as the manager of the band.

According to Scully, there was not a single stick of furniture in
the entire house. There were no lamps, and the only illumination
came from bare bulbs in the ceiling. There were no couches or beds,
so people slept on foam mattresses covered with Army blankets or
Indian fabrics. Because Owsley was doing all the shopping, the re-
frigerator was filled with slabs of meat so huge that he had to re-
move one of the wire shelves in order to hang them in there. Using
a sharp knife, Owsley would cut off slices of beef and fry them up in
a pan for every meal. Along with eggs and milk, this was the only
diet that Owsley allowed everyone who lived there to eat.

His rules about what could be consumed inside the house were
so strict that drummer Bill Kreutzmann's wife, Brenda, had to fight

with Owsley just to get oatmeal for their young daughter. Brenda Kreutzmann soon began derisively referring to Owsley as "a hippie Sonny Bono." Sara Ruppenthal, who was then married to Jerry Garcia, felt the band was being held captive and that Owsley was "obviously a wizard, obviously a madman."

Bob Weir's opinion of Owsley during this period was that he "was both strange and difficult and the soul of kindness. He insisted that we follow his diet regimen, which was basically one hundred percent protein. Meat and milk were all that we were allowed. I was pathologically antiauthoritarian and reacted to that fairly swiftly by becoming a strict vegetarian."

During an era when they were no apparent limits as to how high people could get, the level of drug use within the house was off the charts. In Jerry Garcia's words, "We'd met Owsley at the Acid Test and he got fixated on us. 'With this rock band, I can rule the world!' So we ended up living with Owsley while he was tabbing up acid in the place we lived. We had enough acid to blow the world apart. And we were just musicians in this house and we were guinea pigging more or less constantly. Tripping frequently, if not constantly. That got good and weird."

When Phil Lesh politely declined Owsley's offer to take acid with him one night, Owsley told him, "The band is my body. You are my left leg. My left leg is asleep. You must get high." Knowing it was useless to argue about it, Lesh complied with Owsley's demand. Accurately, drummer Bill Kreutzmann would later write that Owsley "was as stubborn as red wine on a white carpet." After having ingested a synthetic hallucinogen known as STP that Owsley had given him, Kreutzmann stayed awake for seventy-two hours laughing hysterically at all the giant bubbles he saw wherever he looked.

In Bob Weir's opinion, Owsley "had Phil's mind so much that
Jerry wasn't going to fight about it. And if Jerry wasn't going to fight
about it, then I wasn't going to fight it. Billy couldn't give a shit. Billy
saw, 'Here's this guy with some bucks and he's going to bankroll
us.' . . . As far as I was concerned, Owsley was the devil. I'd just as
soon have him living on the top floor than not know where he was."

Weir also told Grateful Dead biographer Dennis McNally that
the name Bear came from the horrifying noises Owsley would make
while he was having sex on the third floor. Whenever Weir would
go up there to tell Owsley that he had a phone call, Weir would hear
what sounded to him like "a combination of a flying-saucer invasion and some sort of demonic hoedown."

Completely unsuited in every way imaginable to communal living, most especially with a group of outsized individuals such as the
Grateful Dead, Owsley was not oblivious to how others in the house
felt about him. "I'll tell you what living with them was like. If
people were on one floor and you were on another and they decided
to go somewhere, the next thing you knew the house was empty.
There was very little concern for others' possible interests. . . . It was
pretty much everybody for themselves. The camaraderie was kind of
gritty. Almost like the Hells Angels, who'd punch each other out and
that made them the best of friends. I never quite understood that."

For someone who needed to control every aspect of what all
those around him were doing, Owsley himself also somehow managed to lose it fairly regularly while the Dead were doing shows in
Los Angeles. After having ingested LSD, DMT, and "something
else" one night before a show, he "saw sound coming out of the
speakers. I thought, 'This is important. I've got to remember what
this is about.' So I studied it very intently, which is difficult to do

when you are that high. I thought, 'This is not what I expected it to look like.'"

At one Acid Test, Owsley was so stoned that he became convinced that one of the Pranksters had found his way into the wiring and was now somehow messing around with the sound. "He came to me completely freaked-out before we started the show," Rock Scully recalled, "and we had to kind of talk him down. Jerry knew what was going on and just sort of looked after his own amp, as did Weir. They just followed the cords and plugged in. But that kind of thing was to be expected at an Acid Test.

"Owsley did have a couple of real weaknesses. At these events, he would get pretty high on his own medicine and become totally preoccupied with something that no one else really cared about. His other great weakness was that he was a fearless and undaunted womanizer who simply would not take no for an answer. He would lay it on thick with women he wanted, and they were either ready for him or scared of him and would run away. But even if they wanted to run away, he would really try to keep them there. If he couldn't, he couldn't. But then he would immediately be on to the next one."

All told, the Grateful Dead's sojourn in Los Angeles lasted for about six weeks. The band performed at Acid Tests held in a Unitarian Church in Northridge, at the Youth Opportunities Center in Watts, at the Sunset Acid Test at Empire Studios, and at the Pico Acid Test at the Cathay Theater, none of which were particularly successful. The band also played two regular shows, one at the Danish Center and another at Trouper's Hall.

With Ken Kesey having decamped to Mexico after faking suicide to avoid going to jail on his latest marijuana bust, the bloom was now most definitely off the rose in the Pranksters' relationship with the Grateful Dead. Because Kesey was no longer around to run the show, the Acid Tests that were held in LA were little more than a pale shadow of those that had come before. Far more significantly, the Pranksters' role as the leaders of the psychedelic revolution had now also pretty much ended.

Putting his own positive spin on the Dead's time of exile in a city where they most definitely did not belong, Owsley claimed, "We all had a good time in LA. We'd go to the beach and do things together. We did our own shows and Acid Tests down there, and every so often we'd get a phone call from San Francisco with a job offer. First, it was a hundred and twenty-five dollars, then one fifty, then one seventy-five, and then two hundred. We had just run out of money, so Rock Scully went to San Francisco and hammered out a deal for three hundred and seventy-five dollars for the Dead to do a show at Longshoremen's Hall.

"In LA, we got constant rehearsal time and we also got to know each other better by living cheek to jowl. But we also created a mystique. Fans of the band were calling promoters and club owners, and they realized the band had a bigger audience than they had thought. So that was the start."

Owsley would never acknowledge the real reason that he and the Grateful Dead decided to leave Los Angeles. Having promised the band that he would not make any LSD while he was working for them, Owsley kept his word until he ran out of money. Converting his remaining stash into pills that he dyed purple to foil the chemical test kits used by police that also turned purple if LSD was present, Owsley made up three thousand doses of acid that came to be known on the street as Blue Cheer.

The well-known journalist Lawrence Schiller was in Los Angeles researching an extensive article about LSD that appeared in *Life* magazine. Schiller was hanging out with four LSD middlemen in their apartment when a girl appeared clutching a peanut-butter jar filled with purple pills. Gleefully she announced, "Look what I got from Owsley." Slipping away, one of the middlemen promptly phoned Owsley at the pink house in Watts to inform him that his cover had just been blown.

As luck would have it, Owsley, Melissa Cargill, and Tim Scully had themselves each just dropped one of those purple tabs only to be told that someone from *Life* magazine now knew all about it. Expecting to hear the sound of approaching police sirens at any moment, the three of them manically scoured the house for LSD and pot. Totally stoned and completely paranoid, they threw everything they found into the trunk of a car and drove to a friend's house on the beach in Venice.

After acting so weirdly that they were asked to leave, they returned to the house only to find the four middlemen waiting for them. Having never before heard of LSD in tablet form, they accused Owsley of having ripped them off. Still high as a kite himself, Owsley told them all to go home and try the stuff. If it was no good, they could come back to work out a deal. Because what they had bought was in fact pure Owsley acid, the middlemen were never seen again.

Although Owsley would later insist "the bit about our leaving Los Angeles because of acid is rubbish—it was only about the band, and nothing else," Bob Weir's version of the story was far closer to what actually happened. "I remember that when we were living in Los Angeles with Owsley and it was time to move, it was very suddenly time to move. He got word that some informant had spilled some sort of beans on him. And so we packed up into a couple of cars and headed north."

After they had returned to San Francisco, someone asked Phil Lesh why they had come back. His succinct reply was, "We were tired of living with Superman."

Jerry Garcia at Olompali with Melissa Cargill in hat and sunglasses as Owsley stands in the background. *(Photo © Rosie McGee)*

9

Olompali

~~~~~

Five weeks after the Grateful Dead had performed at Longshoremen's Hall in San Francisco on April 22 and 23, 1966, the band began living together in a sprawling white mansion that Melissa Cargill and Phil Lesh's girlfriend, Florence Nathan, now known as Rose McGee, had somehow managed to rent for six weeks at the unbelievable bargain-basement price of $1,100.

Located three and a half miles north of Novato in Marin County's Olompali State Historic Park, the idyllic site also featured a swimming pool. With rock luminaries such as Janis Joplin and Grace Slick in attendance along with various members of the Jefferson Airplane and Quicksilver Messenger Service, the house and surrounding grounds soon became a party scene of major proportions where naked teenage girls stoned on Owsley acid frolicked in the sunshine as the Dead played.

Although Owsley had a room of his own at Olompali, he

continued to live in Berkeley and so was "only out there episodi-
cally, and that was where I separated from them." The split was more
than a matter of mere geography. After what they had all been
through together in Los Angeles, both Owsley and the Grateful
Dead knew they could never again inhabit the same living space.
In Berkeley, Owsley was at the center of his own scene and so could
do whatever he liked without having to seek the band's approval.
Yet another factor in the split was the Dead's unwillingness to bow
to what they considered to be Owsley's increasingly impractical
demands.

Although he was now no longer a part of the Dead's daily scene,
Owsley did continue to work as their soundman as the band capi-
talized on their newfound popularity by performing regularly for
Bill Graham at the Fillmore Auditorium and for Chet Helms at the
Avalon Ballroom as well as at a host of other venues where they had
never before appeared.

After he had set up his equipment, Owsley could often be seen
onstage doing what the Dead called "The Bear Dance" as the band
performed. "Owsley liked being part of the band," Rock Scully
would later say. "He liked that a lot. And if he wasn't mixing, he
was dancing. He liked to dance up on the stage and always reminded
us that he was a trained dancer. He also always had his Nagra tape
recorder with him, and there was never any problem with that."

The same could not be said for the new sound equipment Owsley
had purchased through which the Grateful Dead were now playing. Shortly after returning from Los Angeles, Owsley had sold his
Voice of the Theatre speakers and McIntosh MC240 amp to Bill
Graham for use at the Fillmore Auditorium. Being Owsley, he then
bought the Dead "some bigger, even heavier gear."

"It never quite worked," Jerry Garcia would later recall, "and we always had to spend five hours dragging it into a gig and five hours dragging it out afterwards and it was really bringing us down. After going through a million weird changes about it and screaming at poor Owsley and getting just crazy behind it, we finally parted ways, parted company with Owsley. He agreed to turn some of the equipment back into just regular money and bought us some regular standard single-minded equipment so we could go out and play."

By Labor Day 1966, Owsley was no longer working as the sound man for the Grateful Dead. "They decided they wanted to go back to standard amps, and I said, 'Okay, I'll buy you that and in exchange you give me all this stuff. They said, 'Fine.' So they picked out all the stuff they wanted and I paid the bill and took the stuff they had and gave most of it away to the Straight Theater on Haight Street. In terms of our parting ways, it was a bit of everything. It could have been my personality and the sound not being what they had anticipated, but back then I still had a lot to learn."

Accurately summing up what Owsley had done for the Dead during this period, Dennis McNally would later say, "He gave them a vision of quality that quite frankly influenced them for the next thirty years. And that alone gives him credibility for that scene."

By insisting that the band rehearse as often as possible while they had all been living together in Los Angeles as well as urging them to listen to the tapes he had made of their live performances, Owsley had helped the Dead take what they had been doing at the Acid Tests to another level. Out of his own pocket, he had furnished the band with the best equipment that money could buy and then worked tirelessly to ensure that their sound onstage would be second to none. He had also found a manager to look after their business interests, thereby freeing them to focus solely on their music. And perhaps more importantly, he had also imprinted the obsessive nature of his personality on the way in which they approached their live performances.

While anyone else might have been devastated by the loss of the closest personal connection he had ever had with any group of individuals, Owsley took the band's decision in stride. The good news for Owsley was that he was now free to begin making acid full-time once more.

10

Print the Legend

❦

On March 11, 1966, in Laredo, Texas, a federal judge sentenced Timothy Leary to twenty years in prison and a $20,000 fine for having unlawfully transported marijuana across the border while on his way to vacation in Mexico. The incredibly harsh verdict sparked what soon became an overwhelming flood of publicity about what had by then already become the fairly widespread use of LSD in America.

During the next three and a half months, eighty-one articles about the drug appeared in *The New York Times.* Calling the phenomenon "an epidemic of acid heads," *Time* magazine claimed that ten thousand students at the University of California had already taken LSD. On March 25, 1966, the cover of *Life* magazine featured the headline "The Exploding Threat of the Mind Drug That Got out of Control—LSD."

Thirteen days later, a five-year-old girl in Brooklyn was reported to be in critical condition after having swallowed a sugar cube impregnated with LSD that her eighteen-year-old uncle had purchased for $5 in Greenwich Village and then left in the refrigerator. That same day, a Harvard graduate and medical-school dropout who claimed he had been "flying on LSD for three days" was charged with stabbing his mother-in-law to death.

With the media frenzy about LSD now in riotous bloom, the press soon got around to disclosing the role that a man whose name had previously been known only in the Bay Area had played in propagating the drug. Three days before LSD became illegal in California on October 6, 1966, the first full-length account of Owsley Stanley's activities appeared in the *Los Angeles Times*.

Beneath a banner headline on the first page of the second section that read, "'Mr. LSD' Makes Millions Without Breaking the Law—Young Drug Manufacturer Wins 'Acid Head' Set's Applause After Following Checkered Career," George Reasons recounted in great detail the exploits of someone who was so unwilling to let anyone take his photograph that few people outside his immediate circle even knew what he looked like. Two days later, the article was reprinted in its entirety in the *San Francisco Chronicle*.

Without ever having spoken to his subject, Reasons, an investigative reporter who would go on to win a Pulitzer Prize in 1969, began his article by describing how Owsley had sped up to a bank at Sunset Boulevard and Stanley Avenue in Los Angeles on a red motorcycle. Wearing a black leather jacket, jeans, boots, and a white crash helmet, he walked up to the teller's counter and began pulling $1, $5, and $10 bills from his shirt pockets, boots, and crash helmet.

After he had built a "heaping pile of currency" on the counter, Owsley asked the teller to change it all for him into $100 bills. He then walked out of the bank with $25,000 in cash only to come "running back in a panic" after having realized that "he had also pocketed a wad of the bank's money." By the time Owsley returned, bank officials were already calling the police to report the incident.

Unwittingly doing his part to add to Owsley's growing status as a legendary underground figure, Reasons wrote that "even Owsley's close friends and associates do not know his complete name, or his origins. He also has carefully guarded his identity from the world at large." Based on extensive research that included interviews with one of Owsley's ex-wives as well as his father, Reasons accurately portrayed Owsley's life as well as his various brushes with the law before he ever began making LSD.

"What kind of man is he?" Reasons wrote. "By reputation, he is a drifter, a dapper ladies' man, and a professional student." Noting that Owsley himself had recently "dropped from sight," Reasons ended the article by quoting an unnamed police officer who said he doubted that Owsley was still making acid because "with all that money, why should he take the chance?"

In the photograph that accompanied the article, Owsley could be seen in profile in what looked very much like a mug shot or a black-and-white picture that had been culled from a high school yearbook. Wearing a high-collared shirt and a sweater, he is clean shaven and sharp featured. Even with his hair spewing up from his head in a very James Dean 1950s do, Owsley looks preppy and most closely resembles a young Tom Waits. In every way, he seems like an eager go-getter who is destined for success.

After the *San Francisco Chronicle* ran the article under a headline reading, "Home Made Drugs—Strange Story of Bay Area's LSD Millionaire," the Grateful Dead were so amused that they came up

with the song "Alice D. Millionaire," which they sometimes performed live but which did not appear on any of their albums until
many years later. In Bob Weir's words, "I vaguely recall the *Chronicle* headline about 'LSD Millionaire Arrested,' and that is where the
song came from. But it had nothing to do with Owsley. We were
just throwing lines at the canvas, and the title of the song was a pun
that came from the headline, with Pigpen singing lead."

Although this was the first time Owsley would find himself celebrated in song, it would not be the last. Ten years later, Steely Dan
would record "Kid Charlemagne," a song loosely based on Owsley's
exploits that includes a reference to his time in Los Angeles with the
Dead. Owsley is also mentioned by name in "Who Needs the Peace
Corps?" by Frank Zappa and the Mothers of Invention as well as in
"Mexico" by the Jefferson Airplane.

Still living in Berkeley, Owsley had now also rented a house in
Point Richmond, an industrial neighborhood in Contra Costa
County at the eastern end of the Richmond–San Rafael Bridge.
Working alongside Tim Scully and Melissa Cargill in a basement
laboratory there, he had manufactured what may have been more
than three hundred thousand tabs of powerful acid, each of which
contained 270 micrograms of LSD.

On January 14, 1967, more than twenty thousand people showed
up in Golden Gate Park for what was billed as a "Pow Wow—a
Gathering of the Tribes for a Human Be-In." The event featured
an all-star lineup of counterculture luminaries that included Timo-
thy Leary in his first appearance on the West Coast, his former
Harvard colleague Richard Alpert, the poet Lenore Kandel, Jerry
Rubin, Allen Ginsberg, Lawrence Ferlinghetti, Gary Snyder, Michael
McClure, and Suzuki Roshi of the San Francisco Zen Center.

Although the Jefferson Airplane, the Grateful Dead, Big Brother and the Holding Company, and Quicksilver Messenger Service also performed that day, most of those who attended what came to be known as the Human Be-In were there primarily to hang out with one another while tripping on a brand-new batch of acid that Owsley had named while driving into San Francisco to attend the event. "We were on our way back into town from where we had been putting up the acid, and I saw this poster for the 'Pow Wow.' It had an eagle with lightning bolts in its claws and I said, 'We gotta call this stuff White Lightning.'"

As people milled about the park communing blissfully with one another, a masked man whom many mistakenly believed to be Owsley himself floated to the ground clutching a paisley parachute and then began distributing LSD to the crowd. On every level, the foundation had now been firmly laid for Owsley's transmutation into a mythic figure in the counterculture.

Based on the strength and purity of the product he continued to provide to all who wanted it, Owsley was now, in Rock Scully's words, "revered because he was a bit of a guru and an alchemist. He was our good wizard, an extreme Robin Hood–like outlaw wizard. He wouldn't let anybody see his picture so no one knew what he looked like, but he also had a big head. He had no fear of telling girls right off the bat, 'Hi, I'm Owsley. Oh, you've never heard of me? How interesting.'"

Six days after the Human Be-In, Owsley accompanied the Grateful Dead to a show at the Santa Monica Civic Auditorium that featured Timothy Leary as the opening act. Leary would later describe his appearance there as "the high point of the road trip. Hall jammed. Grateful Dead jammed. The LSD alchemist Owsley was everywhere dispensing his White Lightning pills." Owsley himself was less than impressed with Leary's performance that night. "Somebody played a sitar and Tim did a rave and then the band played. He was being Guru Tim."

Tailoring his message to the LA crowd, Leary urged all those in attendance to "flick on the inner switch to full power" to avoid spending "the rest of your life as a badly paid extra in someone else's low-budget black-and-white documentary/training film." As Leary went on and on, Owsley kept pacing restlessly backstage while checking the monitors. Finally, he turned to Tim's companion Rosemary Woodruff and asked, "Are you sure you guys take acid?"

"Everything Tim said that night was very provocative. 'Fuck authorities. To hell with your parents. Turn on, tune in, drop out. Take acid, don't care what anyone will say, do what you please.' He scared a lot of people because they thought he was too weird. And he was. He just kind of went around the bend. Everyone was saying, 'Look, Tim, you're out of control here. You've got to cool it. You're bringing too much heat on everything. We don't want a lot of attention.' But he wouldn't listen."

Owsley had first tried to contact Leary in 1965, only to find himself talking to Richard Alpert over the phone. Owsley then met Alpert while he was lecturing in California, and they soon became friends. In search of the highest possible high one day in Owsley's cottage in Berkeley, Owsley intravenously injected himself, Alpert, Melissa Cargill, and others with pure crystalline LSD. Stoned out of his head, a biker friend from San Jose freaked out and threatened to murder Owsley. Already on the spiritual path that would lead him to becoming Ram Dass, Alpert somehow managed to cool the biker out.

Although Owsley continued to maintain a close relationship with Alpert, he was never able to do the same with Leary. "Unless you were actually kissing Tim's feet, he didn't pay much attention to you. I just tried to be pals with the guy." That Leary had already made himself the public face of LSD use in America was but one of the many factors that kept them apart. Memorably during this period, Owsley told Charles Perry, "Leary may be the king in this chess game but what nobody realizes is that I'm the rogue queen."

Despite his many reservations about the way in which Timothy Leary continued to deliver his relentless sales pitch for LSD, Owsley went to visit him in April 1967. Having already been booted out of Mexico and then the island of Anguilla in fairly rapid succession, Leary and his acolytes were then residing in a four-story, sixty-four-room mansion in Millbrook, New York.

Eighteen months earlier, after having driven across America in their madly painted bus, Ken Kesey and his Merry Pranksters had made the same pilgrimage. What was wildly anticipated by all those on the bus as a summit meeting between the two men who were then the titans of LSD in America turned out to be somewhat of a disaster.

Not at all pleased that Leary was in the midst of a three-day acid trip and so could not be bothered to welcome his visitors personally, the Pranksters began goofing on everything they saw. Ken Babbs, Kesey's right-hand man, went so far as to perform a parody version of *The Tibetan Book of the Dead*, which was considered a sacred text by all those who lived there. As Tom Wolfe would later write, "The clear message was Fuck you, Millbrook, for your freaking frostiness."

After Owsley had driven up from New York City in a rented car with Melissa Cargill, Rhoney Gissen, with whom he had been carrying on an intensely sexual affair for the past two years, and a male friend from California, they all received a similarly lukewarm reception. According to Gissen, Leary seemed far more interested in sipping from a martini than taking any of the LSD that Owsley repeatedly offered him.

Then twenty-six years old, Rhona Helen Gissen had been raised in a well-to-do family in New York's Westchester County. Her father, an observant Jew who attended synagogue each week and laid tefillin every day, was an orthodontist who practiced in the Bronx. Her mother was the president of the local chapter of Hadassah in Mount Vernon.

After having been placed on disciplinary probation during her freshman year at Mount Holyoke College, an exclusive all-girls school in South Hadley, Massachusetts, Rhoney Gissen had transferred to the University of California in Berkeley, where she took LSD for the first time with Perry Lederman.

In what was then his standard approach to any woman to whom he was attracted, Owsley began coming on to Gissen as soon as they met in Lederman's apartment. After Owsley had squeezed a dose of liquid acid onto her tongue from a Murine bottle, they returned to her place, where "they made love till the sun came up." Although Owsley was still involved with Melissa Cargill, he then introduced the two women to one another and they soon became good friends as well as his coworkers. When Owsley called Gissen in New York City to tell her that he and Melissa were coming East to visit Timothy Leary in Millbrook, Gissen happily accompanied them on the journey.

Despite having failed yet again to make any kind of connection with Leary, Owsley's recollection of the visit was relatively benign. "We spent a few days at Millbrook, and I didn't think the people there were a hundred percent genuine. A lot of them were boffing other people all over the place, but they all seemed to have their own agendas. There was a lot of talk and pretension going on, and the only one who seemed to get past that in any sense was Richard Alpert."

High on acid, Owsley and his traveling companions decided to return to New York City on April 4, 1967, to watch the Jefferson Airplane perform at the Cafe au Go Go in Greenwich Village. Having arrived at Millbrook in the dark, Owsley promptly got lost when leaving. Pointing to a New York State trooper named James Dudley, who was sitting in his patrol car on Mill Street, Melissa Cargill told Owsley to ask him for directions to the Taconic Parkway.

After doing so as politely as he could, Owsley drove off, only to realize that the trooper was now following him. Leary's residence in Millbrook had already been busted in a raid led by Dutchess County assistant district attorney G. Gordon Liddy, so virtually everyone seen leaving the estate was automatically under suspicion.

When Owsley failed to signal while changing lanes, the trooper pulled the car over. After Owsley had stepped outside to present his registration, the trooper saw a foil-wrapped packet fall to the ground. Opening it, he identified the substance within as hashish. The trooper then ordered Owsley to open the trunk.

The trunk was packed to the brim with bags and boxes and bottles, most of which contained a wide variety of exotic scents and different kinds of lanolin that Owsley had just purchased in the Kiehl's store on Third Avenue in Manhattan for use in formulating what he called his Barely Burn Bear suntanning lotion. Although no illegal substances were in the trunk, the trooper arrested everyone in the car and took them to jail, where they remained until Owsley got a high-priced attorney in New York to post bail so they could all return to Manhattan.

"I stopped to ask a cop for directions, and he took one look at our hair and, half a mile down the road, he pulled us over and tore the car apart and found what he found. We had to go to court and the judge said, 'You mean, these people stopped to ask you for directions and you tore their car apart?' And he threw it out. It cost me about twenty-five or thirty thousand dollars and I never got any of the money back."

The most serious consequence of the bust for Owsley was that the trooper found the key to a safe-deposit box filled with cash at a Manufacturers Hanover Trust bank in Manhattan. Owsley had already been through another safe-deposit-box nightmare in Berkeley when Melissa Cargill had forgotten the name she had used to rent the box in which five hundred grams of LSD were stashed.

After doing all he could to help her remember the name, Owsley had hired a hypnotist so that Cargill might recall it while she was in a trance. As the hypnotist began leading Cargill up the stairs of Owsley's cottage, she suddenly blurted out, "Missy Stanley," and the missing LSD was then recovered.

The safe-deposit box at the Manufacturers Hanover Trust contained what Owsley would later call "the most cash I ever had in my hands at one time, about $100,000." An enormous sum at the time, which would now be worth seven times that much, all of it was in $100 bills.

Although the charges from the Millbrook bust were eventually thrown out of court, the police never returned the safe-deposit key. Melissa Cargill had a duplicate key, but she could not risk showing up with it at the bank because no one knew if the state police had already notified officials there to immediately inform them if anyone came to open the box.

After Owsley had explained his predicament to Richard Alpert, he set up a meeting for Owsley with Billy Hitchcock. Then twenty-two years old, Hitchcock was the independently wealthy patron who had made it possible for Leary and his followers to live rent-free at his sumptuous family estate in Millbrook. A successful stockbroker at Lehman Brothers, he was the grandson of William Larimer Mellon, the founder of Gulf Oil, and the nephew of Andrew Mellon, who had been secretary of the treasury during Prohibition.

Hitchcock promptly inveigled a lawyer friend named Charles Rumsey to use the duplicate key to retrieve the money. In his apartment the next day, Hitchcock handed all the cash back to Owsley. He then gave it Rumsey, who deposited it all under the name "Robin Goodfellow" in the Fiduciary Trust Company in Nassau in the Bahamas.

Despite Owsley's recollection that the sum of money involved in this particular transaction was $100,000, Stewart Tendler and David May, the authors of *The Brotherhood of Eternal Love: From Flower Power to Hippie Mafia*, would later write that the actual amount was $225,000. "By the winter of 1967," they wrote that Owsley also had more than $320,000 "salted away in safe-deposit boxes around San Francisco" as well as a bank account in London, the contents of which were never revealed. In July 1968, Hitchcock transferred whatever money still remained in the Robin Goodfellow account to the Paravacini Bank in Berne, Switzerland.

According to Owsley, "I literally gave all that money to Billy Hitchcock to keep safe for the community which I had decided owned it although I had not exactly defined who that community was. It was a mental construct, I guess. I requested that he use it to buy gold. He didn't and bought stocks instead. Those that went up, he took, and those that went down, he put against our hundred grand and this went on until it was all gone.

"I thought that with so much money of his own, he would not do this. I was wrong of course. He not only did this but then also became a government snitch who disowned the hundred grand and told the IRS that it was mine. He had already paid the tax on it so they foolishly refunded the money to him and slapped a tax evasion suit on me. In the end, they got nothing as I had nothing left for them to take. And I came to the conclusion that Hitchcock was a weak, dishonorable rat bag."

After they had first synthesized LSD in Los Angeles in 1965, Owsley and Melissa Cargill had returned to Berkeley with eight hundred thousand doses of high-quality acid. Although Bear always insisted that he had then given half of it away, selling four hundred thousand doses on the street at an average price of $3 a dose would have earned him $1.2 million, which would today be the equivalent of more than $9 million.

In Charles Perry's words, "Owsley habitually played it close to the vest but he did give me the impression that he had at least one Swiss bank account when I knew him in Berkeley. I don't know when he would have opened it, probably in 1966, but it might have been even earlier than that." Where all the money that Owsley kept in this account might have gone, no one can say for certain.

Despite having been busted in Millbrook, Owsley had still not been convicted of any drug-related crime and so seemed to those in the counterculture to be truly beyond the law. In a book entitled

America in Legend: Folklore from the Colonial Period to the Present, Richard M. Dorson, a professor of history at Indiana University, would devote ten pages to Owsley's mythic stature as "Mr. LSD," "the Henry Ford of acid," and "the LSD King."

"Anecdotal legends about Owsley, as he was usually called, proliferated throughout the youth drug culture," Dorson wrote. "They celebrated him as a hip-hero manufacturer of the best LSD tablets available, invulnerable to the narcs, the patron of the rock band the Grateful Dead, and a self-made millionaire. Oral legendary traditions about him circulated among street people and college students."

Long before the Internet had been invented, the stories that people shared about Owsley were rarely true but always fantastic. Owsley, it was said, had an electric glow about him but never spoke. He had been seen in Golden Gate Park one day giving away thousands of caps of acid. When the cops came to bust him, all the acid was already gone because Owsley had taken the last ten caps himself when he saw them coming. For him, that was just a normal trip.

Believing that every word they were saying was true, people who had never met Owsley said the reason that he had never been busted was because he was actually a narc who was setting up other people. Someone who had lived with Owsley claimed he had shot strychnine with him. Owsley also put the substance into his acid to make it more intense. Before starting to make acid, Owsley had been a doctor. He was also said to be the son of a wealthy family, a Swede who was now living in exile, and a kid who had just turned twenty.

One Saturday afternoon, Owsley had flown on a helicopter to Mount Tamalpais in Marin County, where he had distributed acid to his disciples like Jesus. In what must still rank as the greatest story of them all, Owsley was said to have gone to visit a group of

Berkeley Free Speech activists who had been thrown in jail. Wearing a purple velvet suit and carrying a Bible, he solemnly began reading passages from it only to reveal that the Bible had been dipped in acid so those in jail could "groove" on the pages. Each activist then tore out a page from a favorite section of the Bible and sucked on it until they were all tripping madly behind bars.

In Dorson's words, "Owsley represents the magician-trickster who can always escape the narcs and whose mind-expanding pills give manna to their takers." On every level, Owsley himself fully understood the process in which he was now involved. "All myths and legends perform sociological functions. They allow people to focus on certain attributes, even if the attributes have nothing to do with the person. Some of that has attached itself to me and some of things are sort of sketchily based on what I actually did.

"I've been made into the hero. The Robin Hood. The John Wesley Harding. The figure who saves the culture but is always just outside the reach of the dark principle. The trickster who changes shape and form. Loki. Hermes. But that was never my plan. Why did Perry Lederman tell people my name? Why did my name attach itself to LSD like glue? I have no idea."

Never one to hide his light under a bushel, Owsley now became even more full of himself than he had been before, if that was possible. John Perry Barlow, who had met Bob Weir while they were both students at the Fountain Valley School in Colorado, first encountered Owsley in June 1967 in the apartment up the street from the Grateful Dead house at 710 Ashbury where Phil Lesh "lived with this incredibly beautiful girl named Florence Nathan, who was always wandering around naked. I was up there one day when this feverish little man came in wearing a blazer with brass buttons on it, and I said, 'That looks like it needs a coat of arms. A family crest, or some damn thing.'"

Picking right up on the suggestion, Owsley told Barlow that he had been "'thinking exactly the same thing at this very moment! And here's what I was thinking. I was thinking about a big *O* made out of flame wrapping itself through the indole ring.'" That Barlow even knew that Owsley was referring to the six-membered benzene ring fused to a five-membered ring containing nitrogen found in psilocybin, serotonin, and LSD speaks volumes about them both at the time. "Owsley said, 'What would you think of that?' And I said, 'That sounds pretty good. Is one of your initials *O*?' He said, 'I'm Owsley.' And I said, 'Well, so far that doesn't mean a great deal to me but it looks like it's about to.'"

Then still pretty much an outsider from the East Coast who had only just arrived in San Francisco, Barlow soon realized that "various people had gotten out on the edge of the framework to the point where if they had gone any further out, they would have been institutionalized." Barlow quickly realized that Owsley's "trip with everybody was adversarial. I was not a rival, but he saw me as a good sparring partner. I don't know if he would have said I was as smart as him, but he might have said I came closer than most.

"For Owsley, there was always a right way and a wrong way. And he was pro-choice. He was magnanimous about it. If you wanted to be an idiot, that was your right. And he was not surprised that you would choose to be an idiot. Because if you did it any way but his, that was pretty much what you were."

Barlow, who over the course of his remarkably Zelig-like life would become close friends with such disparate cultural figures as Timothy Leary and John F. Kennedy Jr., also understood Owsley's desire to remain as anonymous as possible despite his growing no-toriety. "You become as you are beheld. And Owsley was smart enough to know that. Not being photographed was his dodge, which was very thoughtful. He was not so easily beheld. And so there was no caricature for him to live up to. There certainly was one of Jerry Garcia. You become a cartoon of yourself."

And while pride may go before the fall, in truth Owsley was just being who he had always been. Once the Summer of Love in San Francisco became the subject of mass-media attention throughout the nation, it was only a matter of time until he got seriously busted for the first time for making acid.

11

Monterey Pop, and Beyond

~~~~~~

In many ways, the Summer of Love actually began at the Monterey Pop Festival on June 16–18, 1967. With thirty thousand people jamming the Monterey Fairgrounds each day, the legendary performances put on by Otis Redding, Janis Joplin, and Jimi Hendrix immediately catapulted them to a level of stardom they had never before known. Because many of those in attendance as well as the performers were stoned on a brand-new batch of Owsley's acid known as Monterey Purple, much the same could also be said for him. To begin synthesizing the LSD, he had flown to Denver with Melissa Cargill and Rhoney Gissen.

In Denver, Owsley, Cargill, and Gissen were met at the airport by Tim Scully. Their first stop was a dry-ice plant. Picking up several fifty-pound blocks of dry ice, which Owsley called "drice," they drove to a two-story suburban house where Scully had already set

Ravi Shankar, Owsley, and tabla player Ali Akbar Khan backstage at the Monterey Pop Festival, June 16, 1967. (© *Jim Marshall Photography LLC*)

up a laboratory equipped with three custom-made seventy-two-liter condensing flasks and vacuum pumps.

As Albert Hofmann had done many years before him, Owsley was now using flash evaporation to rid his product of impurities. Because LSD was sensitive to ultraviolet light, he replaced all the bulbs in the laboratory with bug lights. Wearing wire-rimmed glasses, masks, paper smocks, and rubber gloves, Owsley, Cargill, Gissen, and Tim Scully did all their work in a soft yellow glow to the music of Buffalo Springfield and Blue Cheer, the hard-rocking San Francisco psychedelic blues power trio who had named themselves after the brand of acid that Owsley had tabbed up before leaving Los Angeles with the Grateful Dead.

After having begun the synthesis, Melissa Cargill flew back to the Bay Area to spend time with Jack Casady, the Jefferson Airplane bass player with whom she was then also having a relationship. Leaving Gissen and Scully behind to continue the work, Owsley went to Los Angeles, where he promised his friend Cass Elliot of the Mamas and Papas that he would provide more than enough acid for the upcoming festival in Monterey. A week later, he returned to Denver, where Gissen and Tim Scully had been "working around the clock" to make as much LSD as they could.

On June 16, 1967, Owsley and Rhoney Gissen flew from Denver to Monterey. Wearing a leather vest and a bear-claw necklace, Owsley was carrying with him one hundred thousand tabs of LSD that had been dyed purple. Half the size of an aspirin, each tab contained 270 micrograms of acid. He also had his Murine bottle filled with LSD, a bottle of dark green hashish oil, and an ounce of powerful *Cannabis sativa*.

Because of the heavy cloud cover in Monterey, the flight was diverted to San Jose. After having boarded a bus heading south, Owsley dosed himself with a drop of liquid acid from his Murine bottle. His first move upon arriving backstage at the festival was to offer a dose to Ravi Shankar, only to have the famed Indian sitar player promptly turn away from him and stalk out of the room.

Nor was this the first time that Owsley had been rebuffed by a world-famous musician whom he was trying to turn on to LSD. Once after having returned to Berkeley from a visit to New York City, Owsley proudly told Charles Perry that he had finally managed to meet "Bobby Dylan." Perry then heard the complete story from someone else who had been there. Owsley had allegedly walked up to Dylan and introduced himself by saying, "Hi, Bob. I'm Owsley. Want some acid?" Dylan's immediate response was "Who is this freak? Get him out of here!"

Unlike Ravi Shankar, many of the other performers at the festival were more than eager to sample Owsley's brand-new batch of LSD. As Pete Townshend of the Who would later say, "Now, at Monterey, Owsley was introducing like Version 7 of his own acid, which up to that point had really only been available in Europe in its clinical variety from Sandoz Laboratories . . . so you knew exactly what you were getting when you took some of it. With Owsley, you had no clue at all. I took some of his at Monterey and I never touched a drug again for eighteen years. It was extraordinarily powerful.

"The thing about Owsley was that when he gave you something, he would take it too. Just to show you. He was like the man who used to eat the king's food. 'Hmm, so you've had some of that? I'll have some, too!' And then he'd go over to somebody else and say, 'Have some acid.' He must have had the most extraordinary liver."

The acid that Owsley was handing out to all who wanted it, as well as some who had no idea what they were ingesting, also caused D. A. Pennebaker's documentary film about the festival to look the way it does. On Saturday night, Chip Monck, who was in charge of lighting at the festival, suddenly realized how tired he was and took what he believed to be a purple heart, the street name for Dexamyl, a widely used form of amphetamine combined with a barbiturate.

"But it wasn't," Monck would later say. "It was Owsley Purple. It was the first time I had taken acid and after it hit, I looked at Laura Nyro and she was going 'Black . . . out.' I was just staring at her thinking it was wonderful. Instead of blacking out the stage. That's why anywhere after Booker T. and the M.G.'s, the Pennebaker film is completely red. I just said, 'Go to frame six, guys—wow, this is fucking groovy.' Pennebaker was not pleased. . . . We went to frame six, we took off our headsets, and we sat there, just sort of gazing at it."

Having already experienced the wonders of LSD in England, John Lennon had become fixated on how he could continue to obtain enough high-quality acid to fuel his creative endeavors. Since money was not an issue for him, Lennon decided to lay in a lifetime supply by going directly to Owsley. The problem was how to get the stuff back into England. Although the film rights to Monterey Pop had already been sold, Lennon sent a cameraman there to shoot the festival for what was ostensibly his own private use. The cameraman's real job was to smuggle the acid back through English customs.

Owsley confirmed his role in this arrangement by saying, "I sent a photographer who had accompanied Brian Jones to Monterey Pop back home with a telephoto lens packed full of Monterey Purple tabs. Jones agreed to share the stash with the Beatles just as they had shared the bottle of White Lightning that Mama Cass had carried over there a few months earlier."

After Owsley's shipment had arrived safely in England, the Beatles spent the next three weeks tripping. The continuing aftereffects of whatever visions they may have derived from Owsley's batch of Monterey Purple can clearly be seen in *Magical Mystery Tour,* the Merry Pranksters–inspired, homemade road-trip movie that the Beatles filmed in September 1967.

Even for Owsley, it did not seem that things could possibly get any higher or wilder. Having been blinded by the insight that the Grateful Dead could someday become even bigger than the Beatles, he was now personally responsible for getting the most popular band in rock history higher than they had ever before been. Being Owsley, he was not yet done turning on rock stars.

Six days after Monterey Pop, Owsley showed up backstage with Rhoney Gissen at Jimi Hendrix's debut performance at Fillmore West in San Francisco. Although Hendrix was surrounded by a circle of friends and family members, Owsley boldly stepped forward and told Hendrix that he wanted to record him while high on acid and playing on his own. Owsley then sealed the deal with Hendrix by lighting up a pipe filled with DMT smeared on mint leaves that they both smoked together.

After the show was over, Owsley and Gissen drove to the Masonic Temple, a large auditorium on California Street in the Nob Hill section of the city. Carrying his tape recorder and a Fender amp, Owsley followed Hendrix into a dark room with heavy draperies and a fireplace. After lighting a fire, Owsley set up his recording equipment and gave Hendrix a dose of liquid LSD from the

Murine bottle. Seated on a chair with his guitar, Hendrix then began to play.

After he was done, Owsley held up the cassette he had just recorded in triumph as Gissen drew the drapes to admit blinding sunlight into the room. Asking if he could see the tape, Hendrix took it from Owsley's hand and threw it into the fire. Smiling broadly, he then grabbed his guitar and walked out the door. Frantically, Owsley did all he could to retrieve the cassette from the fire, only to realize that the tape had already been destroyed.

Lest anyone think that all this could be just another acid-drenched fantasy that never happened, consider that before Jimi Hendrix began his guitar solo on a cover version of the Beatles' "Day Tripper" that was recorded on December 15, 1967, at the BBC-1 studios in London, he can clearly be heard calling out, "Oh, Owsley, can you hear me now?" But by then, Owsley's everyday life had already become far stranger than fiction.

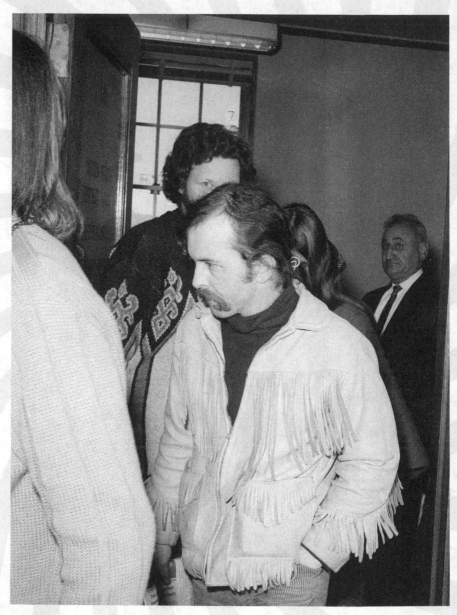

Owsley getting busted in Orinda, California, on December 21, 1967. *(Corbis Images)*

12

Getting Busted

⤸⟡⤸

lthough LSD had now been illegal in California for nine months, it did nothing to stem the invasion of a hundred thousand would-be hippies from all over the United States to the Haight-Ashbury district of San Francisco during the summer of 1967. What had until then been a vibrant and collegial scene soon became a public spectacle of such proportions that a Gray Line bus began regularly driving through the neighborhood so tourists could gaze in wonder at all the long-haired, stoned-out kids who were crowding the streets.

None of what was then happening in the Haight surprised Jerry Garcia in the least. "It was inevitable. I mean, the media portrait of the innocent hippie flower children was a joke. It wasn't that innocent. . . . Stuff like cops and politicians and the rest of the world, all those people just kept right on grinding in the same old groove. So it was not as though any of this was surprising. It wasn't surprising to get busted. It was surprising if you *didn't* get busted."

As always, the Grateful Dead were among the first to feel the heat. On October 2, 1967, eleven people who lived in the Dead house at 710 Ashbury were arrested for possession of marijuana by eight narcotics agents accompanied by a dozen reporters and several television crews. Among those taken into custody in the raid, which became front-page news in the *San Francisco Chronicle*, were lead vocalist Ron "Pigpen" McKernan and Bob Weir, band managers Rock Scully and Danny Rifkin, and Owsley's close friend Bob Matthews. Most of those who were arrested eventually pleaded guilty to lesser charges and paid small fines.

Nonetheless, a message written in capital letters had now been sent. Even in San Francisco, a city where every form of personal eccentricity had not just always been accepted but also actively encouraged ever since the Gold Rush, state and federal authorities were no longer willing to ignore the free-form carnival of drug use that was going on in the Haight.

Two days after the Grateful Dead bust, the Psychedelic Shop closed its doors. On October 6, 1967, the Diggers, who were now known as the Free City Collective, put on an elaborate "Death of Hippie" ceremony. In the weeks that followed, thirty-two truants were arrested in a police sweep on Haight Street. What had begun as an authentic social experiment had, in Charles Perry's words, "collapsed into a monstrous stew of methedrine, heroin, and strong arm crime."

Throughout the Summer of Love, five different street chemists had busily been synthesizing their own versions of LSD, thereby making the Haight, in the words of author Nicholas von Hoffman, "the acid center of the world, the place where it was first mass-marketed and where it is cheapest and most plentiful." During the period between May 1, 1966, and April 30, 1967, the federal Bureau of Drug Abuse Control had already seized about 1.6 million doses of acid.

Fully aware that he was now a high-priority target on the bureau's most wanted list, Owsley continued doing all he could to avoid getting busted. By refusing to ever front his product to others, he was able to keep from having to do business with them again until they had exhausted their current supply. He also insisted on working with only one principal distributor at a time in every market, who would then resell the LSD to dealers on the street. As soon as any of his distributors began to feel that they were under suspicion, Owsley would immediately start working with someone else.

"The change of guard for sales was always a decision based on that person's perception of their situation, not mine. It was always by mutual assessment and agreement. None of us wanted the trouble that we all knew was going to come down the line eventually."

Owsley also devised a practical but ingenious method of safeguarding his product without having to put it into a safe-deposit box. "My regular stash was in a small, inexpensive footlocker, which made a circle between Oakland, San Jose, and San Francisco on the Greyhound bus. I could leave it in the bus station for up to thirty days so I would go to wherever it was, take out whatever I needed, and then send it to myself in the next city. It was always in a safe place and nobody had a clue because I learned early on that if you had a stash, you had to be the only person who knew about it."

Although "the money flow was very embarrassing," Owsley did not "feel it was for me because what I was doing was in my mind a service to the community," and so he "did not buy expensive things, dressed in a normal manner, and drove a second-hand car. In fact, I lived in modest rentals and generally was not much of a consumer."

While it might have seemed this way to him, Owsley had always loved to take his friends out to dinner at restaurants such as Original Joe's in San Francisco, where he would pay for everything they had ordered with $20 and $100 bills from his boots. Despite his penchant for dressing in a manner that Charles Perry described as what "border policemen would later call 'the dealer look,'" Owsley's theory was that "cops don't register outrageousness, only the attempt to be inconspicuous, so if you don't give paranoia an inch, you'll never get busted."

While he was still living in his cottage on Berkeley Way, Owsley had already made so much money from selling LSD that after he had woken up each afternoon and taken an hour-long shower, what Charles Perry called "a regular retinue of petitioners would present themselves like serfs pleading for boons from the king. I can still see Owsley listening warily but regally to their requests, enthroned in the nude on a huge fur-covered chair, drying his hair with the royal hair dryer."

During the spring of 1967, Owsley moved to what became known as the Troll House at 2321 Valley Street in Berkeley. Designed by the Fox brothers, the brick cottage was set back from the street with a cobblestone walkway leading to the front door. Among the cottage's features were a steep, gabled roof, oddly shaped stained-glass windows, a cylindrical chimney, and stucco nooks.

Owsley soon filled the house with what Charles Perry described as "Persian rugs, hi-fi equipment, Indian fabrics, Tibetan wall hangings, pillows, hash pipes, musical instruments made by his personal guitar maker and all sorts of electronic toys like strobe lights." The Troll House soon became "a regular stopover for the psychedelic elite, from Richard Alpert . . . to out-of-town rock musicians."

Adding to the mise-en-scène was the gift that Terry the Tramp brought his old friend one day—a live burrowing owl that Owsley promptly named Screech after what Melissa Cargill had said when she first saw the bird. The owl, which had to be fed a live mouse each week, constantly escaped from its cage and could often be found perched on one of the wooden beams beneath the high ceiling of the living room.

Owsley might well have gone on living in this manner if he had not decided to rent "an ordinary house in a normal neighborhood" at 69 La Espiral Street in Orinda, a suburban town east of Berkeley in Contra Costa County, so he could tab up a new batch of acid that Tim Scully had synthesized in Denver.

"All that was there was a set of screens, lactose, a set of soft lab molds, and unfortunately some crystal acid. We had not yet brought in the press and were just beginning to make the granulation for tabbing. While doing this, we made some soft-molded tabs called 'tablet titrate.' Not a good idea as some of these tabs were smuggled out by one of my friends who sold them to a narc, resulting in the bust."

On December 21, 1967, six agents under the direction of the Bureau of Drug Abuse Control used a sledgehammer to break down the front door of the house on La Espiral Street. They then arrested Owsley, Melissa Cargill, Rhoney Gissen, Bob Thomas, Robert W. Massey, and Owsley's old friend Will Spires on charges of conspiracy to illegally manufacture controlled drugs. After he had sold $3,400 worth of LSD to an undercover agent two days earlier, Spires had unwittingly led the authorities to the house.

Based on the 67.5 grams of LSD that were seized in the house, enough for about seven hundred thousand doses, one agent mistakenly underestimated the street value of the haul at anywhere from $500,000 to $1 million. In fact, it would have been worth about three times that much. Another agent said that Owsley's arrest would probably cause "panic in the streets" because "to a lot of hippies, their idol has fallen."

As Owsley sat handcuffed on the couch after having been given his Miranda warning, he said, "How did you find my place? Even though you have a search warrant, I consider you an uninvited guest in my house." He also told the agents that his LSD formula adhered to federal Food and Drug Administration standards and that he only "made the purest acid for my family and friends."

When agents began seizing the STP that Scully had also made in Denver, Owsley informed them that the substance was still legal and asked them to take only the contraband with them. As one of the arresting agents noted, Owsley was "actually a psychedelic missionary" who "gives the impression that he feels the average person can never actually know himself without turning on with LSD." A day later, all those who had been arrested were freed on $5,000 bail each. In time, the charges against both Melissa Cargill and Rhoney Gissen were dropped.

Not surprisingly, the story of the arrest of the "King of Acid" was picked up by newspapers throughout America. By far the single most astonishing aspect of the coverage was the photograph of Owsley that appeared above a headline in the *San Francisco Chronicle* reading, "LSD 'Tycoon' Held After Orinda Raid."

Just fourteen months after that photograph of him looking young and innocent with short hair had appeared in the *Los Angeles Times,*

Owsley stands with his hands cuffed behind his back in a doorway. With his hair no longer than it was before, he sports the kind of drooping, thick black mustache that was just then coming into vogue.

Although the mustache does make him look somewhat like an outlaw from the Old West, he seems far more like a serious young professor who has only just learned that his research grant has been taken away by those who will never understand the importance of his work. The brief caption beneath the photo accurately sums up his current situation: "Augustus Owsley Stanley Under Arrest—A folk hero of the 'underground.'"

Owsley, now more usually referred to as Bear, in hat and shades with Jerry Garcia at the San Diego International Airport in September 1968. *(Photo © Rosie McGee)*

13

Two Festivals

~~~

In return for 10 percent of what soon proved to be nonexistent profits, Ron Rakow persuaded the Grateful Dead, the Jefferson Airplane, and Quicksilver Messenger Service to perform for free at shows that he began putting on at the Carousel Ballroom at 1805 Geary Boulevard in San Francisco.

The scene at the Carousel Ballroom, an ill-fated attempt to provide an alternative venue to Bill Graham's Fillmore Auditorium as well as the Avalon Ballroom run by Chet Helms on Sutter Street, was so wild and loose that it soon became what Dennis McNally would call "a clubhouse for the city's freak community."

No longer able to synthesize LSD to earn a living because he was now under federal indictment, Owsley and his friend Bob Matthews both began working as sound men at the Carousel Ballroom in February 1968. "I worked for Rakow, but he didn't know what he was doing. We ran three or four nights a week and had a jam on

Tuesday nights with a lot of action, but Bill Graham would tell people that if they played for us, they couldn't play for him, and then he would offer them more money because he wanted the hall himself. Rakow was charging people too little to get in and not paying attention in his typical way, and so it had no possibility of surviving for very long."

On July 23, 1968, Owsley recorded Big Brother and the Holding Company as they performed at the Carousel Ballroom, which had by then been purchased by Bill Graham, who promptly renamed it Fillmore West. Having only just completed *Cheap Thrills*, an album that would become number one on the *Billboard* charts, Janis Joplin and the band were in top form. Finally released in 2012, *Live at the Carousel Ballroom 1968* is now recognized as what Owsley called "the definitive Big Brother live album."

A month later, Dan Healy, who had been mixing the Grateful Dead's live performances, left his job to work with Quicksilver Messenger Service. The Dead, who were then in the studio recording *Aoxomoxoa*, asked Owsley to return to the fold as their sound man. Despite all the travails that they had been through, Owsley was still part of the Dead family. With no other prospects available to him, he quickly accepted the offer.

When the band performed at Fillmore West for three nights beginning on August 20, 1968, Owsley played his part in helping the Dead finally achieve a goal that they had been pursuing with great intensity for more than a year. Convinced that Bill Graham needed to take LSD so he would truly understand what their music was all about, the band had done everything in their power to dose him, but to no avail.

Well aware of what the Dead were trying to do to him, Graham had by then already become so paranoid that he "would never touch anything they gave me. I'd never hug them. Their ladies used to want to kiss me because they had first put a blotter of acid in their mouths. I used to say, 'Kiss the back of my hair if you want.' It became a big running thing." To prevent the Dead from dosing anything that he ate at their shows, Graham also began bringing food from home wrapped in wax paper that he kept in a bag sealed with tape.

Knowing that Graham liked to drink from the cans of soda that he kept in garbage cans filled with ice backstage at Fillmore West, the Dead, in Graham's words, "decided to go for it. What they did, unbeknownst to me, was warn all their people, 'Don't touch any of the soda in our dressing room.' Then they took hypodermic needles and shot acid through the top of every soda can."

Many years later, Owsley explained the Dead's fairly ingenious plan to get Graham high by saying, "Nobody injected anything. We had been trying to hit him for years and we knew he wouldn't touch anything that was opened or in a cup. He had to open his own. We saw what kind of soda he liked and made sure that every can he was likely to find was already fixed.

"When you picked up a soft drink out of a cooler, it was always covered with beads of condensation. So a drop or two was put on the lid of every can in the room. They were all still sealed. The drop was in the little ridge around the outside. Take a sip and the drop went in with the first sip. But it wasn't me who did it. It was our road manager at the time. He was very clever at that."

Totally stoned on acid for the first time in his life, Graham was then asked by Mickey Hart if he wanted to walk out onstage and play with the Dead. Clutching a drumstick in his hand, Graham began wildly beating on a gong before switching over to a cowbell. He then spent four hours onstage. In Mickey Hart's words, "He was in the band. He really was. He was right there. He became one with the universe. And we couldn't stop him. He was possessed. He kept hitting that cowbell like it was the last thing in his life.

"He really lost himself and I think that was when he started to see what it was all about. Once he got high, he saw that we were not just a bunch of hippies getting high and going, 'Yahoo! Look at the colors!' We were serious musicians exploring a new zone. That was something that made an impression on him and he also saw that the Grateful Dead was basically good."

Whenever the Dead were having problems onstage during this period, one of them would inevitably shout out Owsley's name. To remain as anonymous as possible while he was out on bail, Owsley insisted that everyone now begin calling him Bear, which is how he will be referred to from this point on. Now that he was once again mixing their live sound, Bear recorded all the Dead's performances just as he had in the past.

"I always plugged a tape deck into the PA feed to keep a diary of my work, and only for that reason. It seemed to me that since I had already done all the work to produce a mix for the house, why not grab it on tape? The Dead sometimes asked to listen to the show afterwards when we were all still pretty high but I never forced any of them to do this. Left to my own devices, I only ever listened if I'd had problems during the show which was the major practical reason I kept a journal of each show and sound check.

"The comments from the boys were very helpful in my learning how to mix and when they heard the way they actually sounded to the audience, they were stimulated to change things. It was a contributing reason to why they learned how to use dynamics, which are a rarity among loud rock bands, who seem to prefer keeping everything turned up to ten."

Confirming this, Bob Weir told David Browne, the author of *So Many Roads: The Life and Times of the Grateful Dead*, "We used to sit and listen to everything we did and kick it around. . . . That came from his tapes. . . . He instilled in us quality consciousness. If you're going to do something, you have to . . . set your internal compass toward excellence and go for that, because nothing else matters."

By this point in the Grateful Dead's career, the relationship between the band and their audience had already undergone a seismic shift. In Bear's words, "As soon as it starting costing as much as a movie to see a show, the whole thing changed. Instead of people just having a good time and dancing, they stood around mesmerized, staring at the stage as if they missed a stroke of the guitarist's pick, they would really miss seeing something. It became like they were watching a movie, and eventually they even started sitting down and staring at the musicians. Before, it had just been this incredible crazy, wonderful experience, and it was the money that buggered it all up."

As always, the Dead themselves just kept right on working. Finding themselves in dire financial straits early in 1969, the band decided to bring in a real businessman to manage their affairs. Their first choice to fill this position was Bill Graham. Based on his temperament and that he was then viewed as the Antichrist by those in the counterculture who still believed music should be free, his alliance with the Grateful Dead would have been in every sense a marriage made in hell.

At a band meeting in the warehouse the Dead had rented in

Novato in Marin County, Graham and Bear began to argue. Losing his temper, as he almost always did in such situations, Graham demanded that the Dead choose between him and their soundman. After the band made it plain that they were not about to get rid of Bear, Graham stalked out of the warehouse, thereby ending his brief career as their manager.

At yet another band meeting in April 1969, drummer Mickey Hart suggested that the Dead hire his father, Lenny, to manage them. A champion marching-band drummer who had been born Lenny Hartman, he had deserted his wife and young son in Brooklyn and then worked as a drum salesman and a savings-and-loan executive before opening his own drum store in San Carlos, California. By the time Lenny Hart came to the Grateful Dead, he had forsaken Judaism and become a fundamentalist minister.

Although the relationship between him and his son had never been smooth, Lenny Hart persuaded the Grateful Dead that only he could rescue them from their current financial crisis. During a meeting at Phil Lesh's house, Bear told Lenny Hart, "We're doing the devil's work here. Are you sure you want to do this?" Answering yes, Lenny Hart assured everyone that making the Grateful Dead solvent was now his sole mission in life.

Having always disdained all forms of organized religion, Bear was not about to buy into Lenny Hart as the band's new savior. "I never trusted preachers anyway. I came back to the warehouse one day, and this guy was loading our speakers into a truck. I said, 'What the fuck are you doing?' He said, 'Oh, I just bought these from Lenny Hart.' I said, 'No, you didn't. Put them back inside.' Lenny Hart also sold the engine from my MG to a junk dealer, and I never found out where it had gone. He was a piece of shit. He sucked. He was one of those guys like Reverend Billy Graham or Pat Robertson. Fucking creeps."

In April 1969, Bear set up a room at the Dead warehouse where he hoped to record the band playing live. After he had described his vision of using the room as a place where music could be played and studied, Bob Thomas said that this sounded to him like an alembic, a vessel where something could be refined or transmuted as if by distillation. Bear then brought in Ron Wickersham, who had been working at Ampex, and formed a company called Alembic to begin improving the mix whenever the band played onstage.

On May 29, 1969, the Grateful Dead performed with Lee Michaels and the Youngbloods in Robertson Gymnasium at the University of California, Santa Barbara. During an utterly chaotic gig that Michael Lydon would later describe in great detail in his landmark article about the Dead in *Rolling Stone* magazine, Bear could be found lying flat on his back curled up among the amplifiers with his eyes "sightless as fog" as the band began to play.

After having performed for forty minutes through Lee Michaels's PA, Jerry Garcia suddenly stopped playing, ripped out his amplifier cord, and told the crowd that the Dead were now going to set up their own system so "we can hear what the fuck is happening." In a backstage scene that was out of control even for the Grateful Dead, Garcia then began shouting that the band should give everyone their money back if they could not do a "righteous" show.

After having been loudly summoned by Garcia, Bear wandered over to him "still lost in some inter-cerebral space." Garcia then screamed, "Listen, are you in this group, are you one of us? Are you gonna set up that PA? Their monitors suck. I can't hear a goddamn thing out there. How can I play if I can't hear the drums?"

Mumbling that it would take two hours to set up the Grateful Dead's PA, Bear wandered off and disappeared into the night.

By then, the band's roadies had already begun dismantling the PA onstage. Because someone had turned up the houselights, the crowd began to leave. In Lydon's words, "A good night, a potentially great night, had been shot by a combination of promoter burn and Dead incompetence, and at one A.M. it didn't matter who was to blame or where it had started to go wrong. It was too far gone to save the night."

On May 30, the Grateful Dead were scheduled to perform at Springer's Inn, a large dance hall in Portland, Oregon. At seven thirty that morning, Lenny Hart was beside himself as he sat waiting in a car outside the band's motel. Although it was time for the Dead to leave, Bear was nowhere to be found. Drumming his hands against the steering wheel, Lenny Hart demanded, "What's so special about Bear that he can't get here like everyone else?"

Suddenly, Bear appeared looking "sleepy but dapper" in a black leather shirt and vest, pale blue pants, and blue suede boots. Accurately, Lydon described Lenny Hart and Bear as being "like two selves of the Dead at war, with the Dead themselves sitting as judges." Noting that Jerry Garcia had described Bear as "Satan in our midst," Lydon wrote that he was a "friend, chemist, psychedelic legend and electronic genius; not a leader but a moon with a gravitational pull. He is a prince of inefficiency, the essence at its most perverse of what the Dead refuse to give up. They [i.e., Bear and Lenny Hart] are natural enemies, but somehow they have to co-exist for the Dead to survive. The skirmishing has just begun."

When the band arrived at the airport in Santa Barbara ten minutes after their flight had departed, Bear began puttering with his bags as a ticket taker called out for "Mr. Bear." He then went into a long, involved rap about how the Hells Angels really had it down and could use a whip like a stiletto to slice open someone's nostrils, first the right and then the left, just as neat as you please.

After everyone had agreed that the Hells Angels were righteously ugly, the band spent the next few hours hanging out at the airport before finally boarding a flight that got them to Portland in time for the gig. As they all sat in first class enjoying the free drinks while some band members snorted cocaine, Bear proudly displayed the alarm clock he had bought to ensure that he would now always be there whenever the Dead needed to leave. Taking it as a joke, Lenny Hart told Bear that if he was not ready the next time the band had to go somewhere, he would be left behind.

Less than a year later, the Grateful Dead discovered that Lenny Hart had absconded with about $155,000 of their money, a sum that would now be equal to nearly $1 million. The band eventually recovered a third of it, and although they did not press charges against him, Lenny Hart was convicted of criminal embezzlement and sentenced to six months in jail. As a result of this fiasco, Mickey Hart left the Grateful Dead and did not begin playing with them again regularly until 1974.

On June 7, 1969, at the Fillmore West in San Francisco. Janis Joplin came onstage to join Pigpen in a rendition of Bobby "Blue" Bland's "Turn on Your Love Light." Before the show began, a well-known San Francisco acid dealer had dumped what may have been as much as a gram of LSD, worth $50,000 on the street, into a bottle of apple juice backstage.

Cornelius "Snooky" Flowers, the saxophone player in Joplin's new band, got so stoned that he had to be taken to a hospital. Losing all control, Janis Joplin charged over to Bear and began screaming, "You sonofabitch! You dosed my sax player and he's had to go to the hospital."

After the show was over, Bear and Rhoney Gissen left the hall together, only to find Grateful Dead lyricist Robert Hunter lying naked in the street. Stoned out of his mind, he grabbed Bear in a headlock and punched him while shouting, "I will annihilate you, Owsleystein!" (i.e., "Owsley/Einstein"). After getting Hunter into a car, Bear drove him to the dealer's apartment. At dawn, Jerry Garcia showed up to help talk his old friend down from a nightmare trip that Hunter would later say "really did flatten me for a couple of years and made me seriously consider what the wisdom of this drug-taking had been."

What seems astonishing even now is how regularly during this period Bear himself continued to lose it while getting far too high on his own supply. After a performance at Winterland, Mickey Hart and Bill Graham walked back onstage only to find Bear talking to the amplifiers. As Hart told David Browne, "He was saying things like, 'I love you and you love me, how could you fail me?' He was addressing those electronics as if they were a person."

In Bear's words, "I talked to the amps a couple of times. During one show, I was hanging on the curtain because I couldn't get away from the amps, which sounded to me like the explosion at the end of the world. I could smell the smoke of the universe as we knew it collapsing, and I didn't want to leave because I was too afraid. Bill Graham carried me outside and put me in his car. I had been taking too many things and I blew it and just got carried away."

With the Dead now performing at "a lot of festival style shows where the equipment would all wind up at the back of the stage in a muddle," Bear found himself having to "spend a fair amount of time moving the pieces around so we could read the name on the boxes. I decided that we needed some sort of marking so we could identify our stuff from a distance."

While driving to the Dead warehouse in Novato one day in his MG, Bear saw a sign on a building along the freeway that featured a blue-and-orange circle with a white bar across it. Thinking it would be cool if the circle were red and blue and the white bar were a lightning bolt, Bear told Bob Thomas about it, and they then had someone spray-paint a logo that "was a quick way of marking our gear and that you could spot from anywhere."

A few days later, Bear suggested to Bob Thomas that "perhaps the words 'Grateful Dead' could be placed under the circle, using a style of lettering that would appear to be a skull if you saw it from a distance." Thomas said, "Oh, that's a good idea," and "a few hours later he came down from the loft with the design." The Steal Your Face logo, aka the Stealie, has since become one of the most well-known trademarks in the history of rock.

Despite having come up with the idea for the basic design, Bear was never compensated for what he had done. "I didn't get anything from it. It was my concept and Bob Thomas's artwork, but he sold it to the Grateful Dead in 1969 for two hundred and fifty dollars for use as a letterhead. Are you kidding me? That's the most powerful corporate logo that has ever been designed, and I've looked at them all. It should be in the Museum of Modern Art in New York."

The logo was on the Grateful Dead's equipment when they took the stage at the Woodstock Music & Art Fair at ten thirty at night on August 15, 1969, to play before a crowd of four hundred thousand people. Long before the band began a performance that, in

Dennis McNally's words, "would rank in their memory as one of their worst ever," the setup itself was plagued with problems.

To move each band's equipment on and off the stage as quickly as possible, festival organizers had mounted large plywood circles on casters so everything could be rolled into place. From the moment he first laid eyes on them, Bear was convinced that they were a disaster in the making. "We arrived at Woodstock and saw these big cookies, and I said to Michael Lang, 'This doesn't work.' He said, 'What do you mean it doesn't work?' I said, 'Our equipment is too heavy. This thing won't hold us up. We have to set our stuff up on the stage itself.' He said, 'Absolutely not. You have to do it this way.'"

After Bear and the other Dead roadies had set everything up on the plywood circle, the stagehands "hooked ropes up to it and turned the thing around and it moved approximately one foot and all the casters broke. *Wham!* All the two-by-fours ripped out, and down came the thing onto the stage. So we had to take everything down and set it all back up again, and that took like twenty minutes. Everyone was bitching that it was our fault, but it wasn't."

Once all the gear had been hooked back up, Phil Lesh plugged in his bass guitar and "out came the sound of the helicopter radio. I said, 'Take our cable and the PA cable and ground them all to the same one the helicopter is grounded on,' but they didn't want to do that. I said, 'You either do this or the band is not going to play.' I stopped the show because Phil had told me that he wasn't going to play with the helicopter radio coming out of his amplifier."

After Bear had shown the first-class radio operator's license he always carried around with him in his wallet to the festival's electrician, he finally agreed to do this "and there were no more problems. The band came out and I went to the booth and it was not a good show. We were real tired and it was late and there was too much hassle and sitting around. Those shows were not easy."

For the Dead, this show proved to be far worse than any of them could have imagined. By the time the band took the stage, rain was pouring down in sheets. The wind was blowing so hard that holes had to be cut in the light-show screen to keep it from hauling the stage off its foundation like a giant sail. When Bob Weir leaned into his microphone to begin singing, a huge blue spark struck him in the lip and knocked him backward. As Jerry Garcia left the stage, he told Jon McIntire, the band's road manager, "It's nice to know that you can blow the most important gig of your career and it doesn't really matter."

Despite how badly the Grateful Dead had performed at Wood-stock, Bear himself had a fine time at the festival. Staying awake until Jimi Hendrix ended the event, Bear happily dispensed liquid LSD from his ever-present Murine bottle to one and all. His opinion of the festival itself, however, was far less favorable: "The wrong sorts of people got control of it and made it into a disaster. Instead of just flowing with it, they tried to control everything. All those weird announcements about things that could have been easily avoided."

Perhaps the single most notable announcement made from the stage at Woodstock was Chip Monck's gentle warning that "the brown acid that is circulating around us isn't too good. It is suggested you stay away from that. Of course it's your own trip. So be my guest, but please be advised that there is a warning on that one, okay?" High as a kite on his own LSD at the time, the message was most definitely not one that Bear wanted to hear.

Less than two months later, Bear appeared in the US District

Court in San Francisco alongside Robert Massey, Bob Thomas, and Will Spires to stand trial for the bust at 69 La Espiral Street in Orinda. After a nonjury proceeding in which the government's entire case against Bear "seemed to hang on a single fingerprint found on confiscated laboratory equipment," Judge William T. Sweigert chose to believe the expert witness who testified that the print belonged to Owsley.

Rejecting the somewhat ludicrous claim offered by the defense that Bear had been manufacturing LSD at the house strictly for his personal use, as well as numerous technical challenges concerning the legality of the search warrant that federal agents had obtained before raiding the premises, Sweigert found all four defendants guilty on charges of possessing, manufacturing, and conspiring to make and sell LSD.

On November 7, 1969, Sweigert sentenced all four men to three years in jail and ordered each to pay $3,000 in fines. Bear's high-priced lawyers immediately filed an appeal that began wending its way through the Ninth Circuit Court.

Twenty-four days later, on Monday, December 1, 1969, the Grateful Dead performed at the Grande Ballroom in Detroit, Michigan. Having already decided that marijuana could only properly be smoked in joints that had been rolled in Chanticleer papers, a brand that could then only be bought in Canada, Bear drove across the border to Windsor, Ontario, where he purchased a gross of them.

On his way back to Detroit, American customs officials opened the trunk of Bear's rented car and discovered that it was stacked to the brim with packets of rolling papers. "They found that suspicious," Rock Scully would later say, "and so they looked all over for the dope and there wasn't any, but it was obvious to them that this guy was a doper so they followed him back to the hotel and immediately began going through all the rooms trying to find him.

"Expecting to bring some queen of the underground there, whenever Bear checked into a hotel room, he would set up Indian madras and paisley blankets on his bed and change all the lightbulbs to black lights and bulbs that flickered like candles. He would burn this patchouli incense so the room was always filled with smoke and looked like an old San Francisco bordello. He would also take the dresser apart and use it as a workbench and unfold this pantheon of tech gear, soldering guns, and scopes from his briefcases, and so his room was always bizarre beyond belief.

"When the cops finally entered Bear's room, it was all just so confusing for them because they couldn't turn on any of the lights and Bear refused to be intimidated by them. 'What do you mean? Of course, I bought cigarette papers! I can't find them anywhere and I'm taking them home to California with me!' I think we only avoided a bust there out of their sheer confusion. I just thanked my lucky stars that Bear was clean, because otherwise the cops would have gone through all our rooms."

Bear then ended what had already been an eventful year not just for him but the counterculture as well by setting up the sound system at Altamont Speedway in Alameda County for a massive free concert featuring the Rolling Stones on December 6, 1969. "I knew well ahead of time that we were heading into something that was not going to be easy, but I was committed. I took seven absolutely unrelated sound companies, each of which was run by a guy with an ego as big as the Eiffel Tower, and put it all together into one functional unit. The reason I was able to do this was because I was the only person who had worked with every single one of those different kinds of sound systems."

On the day before the concert, Bear was driving to the site over the Altamont Pass with Dan Healy. "We looked up, and all of a sudden there was this rocket blowing up in the sky and I said, 'That's got to be a strange sign.' We couldn't figure where to get off the freeway, so we took a turnoff and the road kept getting weirder and weirder and the trees kept getting closer, and eventually we went through some kind of tunnel and came out into the backyard of this place.

"It was like a moonscape of crushed auto bodies, and as we drove along, we looked over to the left and saw this place that looked like a skull. It was the actual arena where they held these demolition derbies, and I thought, 'Oh my God, this place smells like death. This is where people come to watch drivers crash their cars into one another while hoping one of them might die.' And I realized that if you took acid at this show, you were going to have a trip you didn't really want."

Bear then "took just the tiniest amount, and because of that, I was able to understand what was happening without being controlled by it. I watched a Hells Angel punch out Marty Balin of the Jefferson Airplane onstage, but I knew we couldn't control any of it." Because there was only enough scaffolding to build a stage three feet high, and all those at the front of the crowd of three hundred thousand people kept pushing forward, the Hells Angels who had been hired to provide security began using sawed-off pool cues to beat them back.

Having wisely decided not to perform at Altamont that day, the

Grateful Dead had already left the site by the time the Rolling Stones finally took the stage. As the Stones began to play "Under My Thumb," a seventeen-year-old black man named Meredith Hunter began waving a pistol in the air. In full view of the film crew shooting the documentary that would be entitled *Gimme Shelter*, Meredith Hunter was stabbed to death by a Hells Angel, who was later acquitted of the crime.

To the straight media, the free concert at Altamont was the death knell for a counterculture that had only been born just four short months earlier at Woodstock. The Rolling Stones, who were then considered the bad boys of rock, were widely reviled for having ever believed the Hells Angels could police anyone, much less themselves. Bill Graham would later call the event "the Pearl Harbor of rock."

Yet another casualty of that day whose passing went pretty much unnoticed was Terry the Tramp. By then, he had attained such legendary status that when Cream had come to play the Fillmore for the first time in 1966, Terry the Tramp was one of the people whom lead guitarist Eric Clapton was most impressed to meet. Described by Mountain Girl as "the most fop of all the Angels," Terry the Tramp, in Kesey's words, "wore more stuff and had more stuff hanging off him and he could just shake it all around."

After he had seen a show by the Doors that left him less than impressed, Kesey walked out into the lobby of the Fillmore Auditorium one night and found Terry the Tramp standing there "loaded to the gills" on acid. When Kesey asked him what he thought of the Doors, Terry the Tramp replied, "Gettin' smaller all the time. Gettin' smaller all the time." And so they were, but in ways that no one back then could even begin to understand.

Blamed by many of his fellow Hells Angels for having involved them in the media disaster that Altamont became, Terry the Tramp killed himself in Bear's house in the Oakland Hills by taking an overdose of Seconal on February 13, 1970. He was thirty years old.

14

Set Up Like a
Bowling Pin

⁘

After the Grateful Dead had performed two shows in the Honolulu Civic Auditorium on January 23 and 24, 1970, Bear spent a few days in Maui before flying back to San Francisco and then on to New Orleans, where the band was scheduled to open a brand-new venue known as the Warehouse along with the Flock and Fleetwood Mac on January 30.

In May 1969, bass player Jack Casady of the Jefferson Airplane had been busted for possession of marijuana in New Orleans, and so the Dead had already been warned to be careful while they were there. After being provided with the name of a local attorney when they landed at the airport, the band checked into the same hotel at 300 Bourbon Street where Casady had been arrested.

A house detective at the hotel stopped Pigpen and asked him if he was with the Flock. When Pigpen told him that he played with

Less than two weeks after having been busted in New Orleans, Bear stands behind the amps at Fillmore East on February 11, 1970. (©*Amalie R. Rothschild*)

the Dead, the house detective said, "Look, you better be clean because you're going to get busted." Although Pigpen then relayed this warning to Jon McIntire, the road manager dismissed it as just part of the vocalist's ongoing paranoia about both cops and drugs.

After a less-than-stellar show at the Warehouse, the Dead returned to their hotel sometime after 3:00 a.m. and gathered in the room shared by Bob Weir and McIntire. Someone had already shown up with what Dennis McNally later described as "a pound of pot and a goodly quantity of hashish." McIntire was busily cleaning the marijuana when the New Orleans Police Department narcotics squad came through the door.

Having obtained a search warrant at 1:50 a.m. on the basis that "opium derivatives, amphetamines, barbiturates, marijuana, synthetic drugs, and narcotics paraphernalia" were present in Room 2134 of the hotel, the cops promptly arrested Jerry Garcia, Bob Weir, Phil Lesh, Bill Kreutzmann, Jon McIntire, two Dead roadies, an assortment of partygoers, and, most grievously for all concerned, Bear as well. The subhead on the front-page story that appeared in the *New Orleans Times-Picayune* the next day read, "Rock Musicians, 'King of Acid,' Arrested."

Despite all available evidence to the contrary, Bear would insist to the end of his days that the bust had come about because of a vendetta that was being waged against him by the promoter of the New Orleans Pop Festival in Baton Rouge, with whom Bear had gotten into a knock-down, drag-out argument six months earlier. "The promoter set us up to get busted. The cops came in and they not only found stuff, but they also brought stuff and planted it too. That was what ended my touring with the Dead. Bad, bad time for me."

Bailed out eight hours after they had been arrested, the Dead returned to the Warehouse and played what everyone agreed was a far superior show than their set the night before. The bust was eventually laid to rest when Joe Smith, the Yale-educated A&R manager who had signed the band to Warner Bros. Records, called Jim Garrison, the noted John F. Kennedy assassination conspiracy theorist who was then the district attorney of New Orleans. In return for Smith's generous offer to contribute $50,000 to Garrison's campaign fund as well as his heartfelt promise that the Grateful Dead would not return to New Orleans anytime soon, all the charges were dropped.

Although the band had been set up like a bowling pin in New Orleans, the Dead went right on working. Because Bear had been arrested two weeks after the period of time during which he was permitted to be outside the jurisdiction of the Ninth Circuit Court in San Francisco, his bail was revoked on February 27, 1970, and he was sent to jail.

After somehow getting himself back out once more, Bear was then busted yet again with Bob and Betty Matthews on July 15, 1970, at the house in the Oakland Hills where they were then all living. The warrant for the arrest had been issued at the request of Bear's landlord, who went to the police after it became evident to him that Bear was not about to vacate the premises on the day that he had been told to do so. The ensuing police search turned up marijuana, hashish, and "a tiny bit of opium."

On July 21, 1970, Bear's bail on the Orinda bust was revoked once more on the grounds that he was "a threat to the community and a flight risk." Despite being urged by Rhoney Gissen to flee to Canada to avoid going to jail, Bear "accepted that it was his duty as an American citizen to do time" and "refused to run away."

Not long after he had been returned to jail in Oakland, Bear told Gissen over the phone that he had been assaulted by a fellow inmate, who had broken Bear's nose with a punch. Although Bear had insisted that he needed plastic surgery, the staff doctor handed him a Band-Aid instead.

Then already nearly four months pregnant with Bear's child, Rhoney Gissen could not visit Bear in jail because of her involvement in the bust in Orinda. In order to do so, she then managed to circumvent this restriction by obtaining a borrowed ID. To her, he looked thin and depressed. While she was helping Melissa Cargill move all of Bear's stuff out of the house in Oakland Hills, Gissen learned that Cargill was also pregnant. Taking turns using the borrowed ID, both women then regularly went to see Bear in jail.

On October 4, 1970, Janis Joplin, then twenty-seven years old, died of a heroin overdose in the Landmark Motor Hotel in Hollywood. After learning in jail of Joplin's death, Bear wrote an incredibly touching eulogy for her by hand on a page of lined notebook paper. Entitled "Notes on a Lady," the eulogy began by stating that not only were he and Joplin both Capricorns, but they also shared the same birthday. As Edgar Allan Poe, Robert E. Lee, Cézanne, and Richard Lester, the director of *A Hard Day's Night* and *Help!*, had also been born on January 19, Bear reckoned that this had to be a weird day to be born.

Admitting that he and Joplin had most certainly had their differences, Bear wrote that he loved her. Although he had tried to share his LSD with her, she had always preferred a slug of whiskey straight from a bottle of Southern Comfort to ease her pain. Concluding his eulogy, Bear wrote that he knew she was scared and trying to hide while fighting some kind of phantom that would disappear in the light but that she herself had never done so.

Two and a half months later, on December 21, 1970, Rhoney Gissen gave birth to a son. A few days later, she took the baby with her to visit Bear in jail, where he named the baby Starfinder. About three weeks later, Melissa Cargill gave birth to a girl, whom Bear named Iridesca, but who came to be called Redbird.

After having languished for months in a county jail that in many ways was a far more difficult place to do time than a federal prison, Bear was transferred to the Terminal Island penitentiary in San Pedro, California, to begin serving his three-year sentence for manufacturing LSD. A low-security federal correctional institute on a man-made island in the San Pedro harbor, the prison had formerly housed Al Capone, famed LA racketeer Mickey Cohen, and Charles Manson, who had been incarcerated there in the sixties for stealing cars and trying to cash a forged check. In 1974, both Timothy Leary and G. Gordon Liddy, the convicted Watergate conspirator who had busted Leary in Millbrook, would also find themselves there.

"At Terminal Island," Bear would later say, "they tried to put me into the metal shop, where you had to work your ass off. I'd had some injuries to my fingers as a kid, and so I used my acting training and freaked out and said I was terrified of sharp metal things because the ends of my fingers had been cut off.

"So then they said, 'We've got either the grounds, where you can be a gardener, or food service.' And I said, 'Oh, I like working outside.' And they said, 'You're in food service.' Which was exactly where I had wanted to go. I was still eating only meat, and so in food service I could completely control my diet.

"I worked my way up to the top job, which was as a linebacker for the steam tables, and I traded my two cartons of cigarettes a week for a steak a day from the butcher, and I got all the meat and eggs I needed and cooked my own food and had a great time."

As Timothy Leary would also do when describing his experiences in prison, Bear always portrayed his time behind bars as a series of personal triumphs in which he got the best of not only his jailers but also all those with whom he was now confined. However, as Bear would later tell David Gans, "I had a hard time at the beginning because I kept telling them that I didn't do it for the money. I was just doing it because of service to the community.

"As long as I maintained that, my time was hard. I got shit from everybody. As soon as I stopped saying that, they assumed I did it for the money and I acquiesced, no problem then. That was the only reason you were allowed to be in prison, because you did it for the money. If you did it for any other reason, you were lying."

Having only ever lived communally with the Grateful Dead, Bear now found himself surrounded by about a thousand other inmates. Remarkably, the Dead came to visit him at Terminal Island on August 4, 1971, so they could perform in the prison library. Bear helped the band's roadies, all of whom were high on acid, set up gear that the authorities had not even bothered to search as it had come through the gates. He then introduced them to some of his fellow prisoners. Bear also told one of the Dead's roadies that he had to get back out on the road with the band again.

As perhaps some form of acknowledgment as to why Bear was now in the audience rather than onstage with them, the Dead began their twenty-song set with "Truckin'." In the *Rolling Stone* interview that Jann Wenner and Charles Reich conducted with Jerry Garcia that fall, which was then published in book form, the Dead's lead guitarist went on at length about Owsley in a way he would never have done if the man he was talking about had been there. Knowing Garcia, he might well have done this specifically to boost the spirits of someone who he knew would be reading his words behind bars.

Garcia said that getting to visit Bear at Terminal Island had been "just great. Owsley is a hero. I didn't get a chance to get into a really in-depth thing with him, which I was sorry about, but his head's together, he really feels good. And he's doing what he feels he has to do, I suppose. And I'm looking forward to having him out again. He's a tremendous asset when he's working.

" . . . I think that there's an important lesson involved which took us a long time to snap to, which is this: Owsley is the guy who brought a really solid consciousness of what quality was to our whole scene. And that's been the basis of our operations since then: being able to have our equipment in really good shape, our PA really good, stuff like that.

"We try to display as much quality as possible in the hopes of being able to refine what we do. And that's the thing Owsley does like no other human being that I know can do or devote his attention to, and that is that thing of purification. It's a real thing with him. He's really, really good at it. Owsley's a fine guy. He's got just an amazing mind.

"He's got enough of every kind of experience, man! There's almost nothing the guy hasn't done. You know he's a licensed blacksmith? Not only that, but he's got a first-class broadcaster's license, too. He worked for years in TV. He's also an excellent auto mechanic; he's obviously a chemist. There's almost nothing he doesn't do, or at least have a good grasp of. He understands just about every level of organization. He's just incredible, he's got some incredible capacity for retaining information."

Sometime after the Dead had performed at Terminal Island, Bear was transferred to the low-security federal correctional institute in Lompoc, California, not far from Vandenberg Air Force Base. "When I went to Lompoc, I stayed in food service, but they cooked it all up inside the big prison so I wound up taking care of the dining room, and I figured out a way of keeping the floor absolutely shiny by only having to clean it once a week.

"Then they put this black guy in there who insisted on doing it his way, and he fucked it up. I had a private talk with the guy and I realized, 'I've gotta get out of here. This guy is going to kill me.' It was also too much work, so I transferred into the maintenance shop, and that was when I got into art. I had access to the tools and I began carving pieces of wood and stone. There was a lot of great serpentine lying around in Santa Barbara County, and then I got into using welding torches so I learned how to do all kinds of stuff."

When Charles Perry went to visit Bear at Lompoc, the prison reminded him "of my high-school campus except you couldn't go home after sixth period." Although Perry's name had been announced at the beginning of the hour set aside for visitors, Bear did not appear until the assigned period of time was nearly over. Arriving out of breath, Bear handed Perry a belt buckle he had made for him, "a lion's head boldly composed of a few drops of molten brass."

By then, Bear had already smuggled in tapestries for his cell as well as "all sorts of hi-fi and electronic equipment." The smaller objects had been handed to him out on the visitors' lawn, while the bigger items such as tape decks had been hidden beneath a pew in the prison chapel. As Perry would later write, "The joke around

Lompoc was that when Owsley was released, he'd have to leave in a Bekins van."

The next time Perry went to visit him at Lompoc, he conveyed the news that *Rolling Stone* magazine wanted to publish an interview with Bear. By then, Columbia Records had issued an album of Janis Joplin performing live in concert that included three tracks that Bear had recorded at the Carousel Ballroom. Although Bear had been paid for the work, the label had remixed what he had done. In exchange for doing the interview, Bear demanded that the magazine print an item stating that "word was out on the street" that there was "something funny" about the mix.

Although Perry persuaded a San Francisco disc jockey to say this on the air and the item then ran in the magazine, Bear changed his mind about doing the interview because *Rolling Stone* was only interested, in Perry's words, "in his drug career and the interview would caricature him as a mere chemist and a has-been." Instead, Bear offered to write an essay on Marshall McLuhan's theories, which he wanted to sign Publius. Not surprisingly, the magazine declined his offer.

While doing the rest of his time with Bob Thomas, Will Spires, and Robert Massey, all of whom had been convicted with him in the Orinda bust, Bear also worked in the prison laundry and was then put in charge of the gym, where he began regularly lifting weights.

After completing two years of his three-year sentence, Bear was released from prison on July 15, 1972. Since it was her weekend to visit him, Rhoney Gissen came with their eighteen-month-old son, Starfinder, to pick Bear up in his royal-blue Mercedes 190. He then began driving north on Highway 1. They stopped to have lunch on the patio at Nepenthe in Big Sur, but when someone there recognized him, Bear decided to leave without eating. After arriving in the apartment that Gissen had rented in Berkeley for the week, she went out with their young son to shop for food. When Gissen and Starfinder returned, Bear was gone.

On August 21, 1972, Bear rejoined the Grateful Dead as they performed onstage at the Berkeley Community Theatre. Although he had survived his time in prison, Mountain Girl would later tell David Browne that when Bear began working for the band again, he seemed "completely changed, and not in a good way. He was dark and dour. He'd lost most of his sense of humor. Prison was hard on him."

Having attained a brand-new level of popularity after the release of their wildly successful *Workingman's Dead* and *American Beauty* albums, the Grateful Dead were now regularly playing stadiums rather than the theaters and ballrooms where they had performed before. In John Perry Barlow's words, "The scene was completely different when Bear came back from prison. That was a mutagenic couple of years. Hell, we all thought it had been a long strange trip in 1969. We didn't know anything about long or strange. Bear just had a difficult time not being in an autocratic position anymore."

By far the single most difficult thing for Bear to accept was that the road crew, whose drugs of choice had now become cocaine and beer, were all performing separate and distinct functions while the band was onstage.

"The thing that had changed while I was locked up was that it had all become partitioned. The guys onstage had little black curtains between their little cubbies and it became, 'This is my territory, that is your territory, this is my job, that is your job.' People had stopped hanging out together backstage and had started going into their own dressing rooms before shows, and everyone had their own little cubicles onstage, and when I came back out of the joint, all that was absolutely alien to me.

"Whether or not cocaine was the source of that, I don't know, but that was what I experienced. A bunch of individuals and more of a star trip. Somebody told me, 'We're much more professional now.' Weren't we always professional? I mean, we had been writing the book on what that meant in rock 'n' roll."

Although Phil Lesh, who had always been Bear's staunchest supporter in the Dead, felt that the band now had "three really strong skill sets working together" with Bob and Betty Matthews mixing the sound in the house, Dan Healy as "the supremo hands-on troubleshooter," and Bear as "the wild-eyed radical visionary man," the problem was that "each of them wanted some of the other's turf. Both Healy and Bear, for example, wanted to mix real-time."

Bob Weir saw that "there was a lot of water that had gone under the bridge during the time Bear was in prison in terms of our development, particularly in regards to the equipment we were using and our approach to it, so he had a lot of catching up to do. And he disagreed in a major way with some of the direction in which we had chosen to go, and he was capable of being fairly bullheaded."

In Bear's words, "I found on my release from jail that the crew, most of whom had been hired during my absence, did not want anything changed. No improvement to the sound, no new gear, nothing different on stage. They wanted to maintain the same old same old which under their limited abilities, they had memorized to the point where they could sleepwalk through shows. Bob Matthews, who had been mixing since my departure, did not want to completely relinquish the mixing desk, which was a total pain in the ass for me, since he was basically a studio engineer and no match for my live mixing ability."

Despite having spent the last two years in prison, Bear was also offended by the profane language the crew now regularly used and went so far as to gather them all together to say, "I'm used to working with my friends. I don't want to work with people who use language like you guys do." Not surprisingly, his heartfelt plea fell on deaf ears.

The confrontation that had been brewing between Bear and the rest of the crew was not long in coming. When Bob Matthews did not show up for a university gig in the fall of 1972, Bear persuaded some local college kids to help him load out the gear, only to then discover that one of them had taken the mixing board to his dormitory room.

After the crew blamed Bear for this at a meeting before the next gig, words began to fly. The argument got so heated that one of the Dead's roadies picked Bear up and threw him across the room into a watercooler. Bear then went to the band and asked that he be given the power to hire and fire the crew so they would all know that they were now working for him.

"I said to the band, 'Look, it doesn't mean that I'm going to fire anybody, but I want the power to fire everybody and then hire them back so they'll know they are dependent on me for their jobs, and that if I need something done, they have to listen to me. Because if I have to be dependent on them, they just say, 'Fuck you. I don't want to do that.' And the band wouldn't do it. Instead, they marginalized me."

Bear described the limbo in which he now found himself to

Dennis McNally as "Here's a piece of your job back, just a taste—
and stand over there." In McNally's words, "He wanted to be the
soundman and he was not the soundman, and he never got this
because he had a single vision. That was his strength and his flaw.
If everyone would have gone along with that, fine. In this case, they
didn't.

"You had a bunch of macho cowboys as crew who were snort-
ing blow and drinking a whole lot of beer, and here was Bear, who
was offended by their language and offended by their beer, and
he was tiny. Most of the crew were big guys, and Bear was about
five feet six inches tops and weighed about a hundred and forty-
five pounds, so it was not as though he had this imposing physical
presence."

Although Bear continued working for the Grateful Dead for the
next three years, he did so primarily to earn enough money to keep
his head above water. As the band became increasingly fixated on
the way they sounded in concert, they finally decided that only Bear
could devise the kind of system they were dreaming about. The band
then authorized him to construct what would become the single
greatest technical achievement of his career.

15

Wall of Sound

❦

On September 3, 1972, the Grateful Dead performed before sixty thousand people at Folsom Field, the football stadium at the University of Colorado in Boulder. During the show, a huge lightning storm began. In John Perry Barlow's words, "Bear had a whole bunch of notions about electricity, and one of them was that the stage should always be grounded to itself, thereby becoming what is called a 'floating ground.'

"Once this huge electrical storm started, the energy potential of the stage was different from its surroundings, so we literally had Saint Elmo's fire on everything. Balls of lightning were rolling around the equipment, but the band went right on playing while standing in two inches of water. There was a big canopy over the stage and we ripped holes in that because of the wind, so the water onstage just got even deeper.

"At one point, some madman with an electric Skilsaw in his

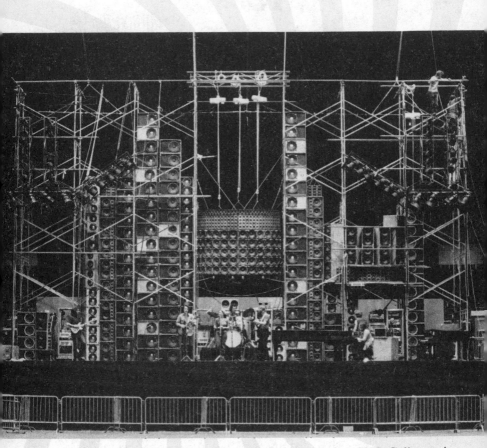

The Wall of Sound in all its awesome splendor at PNE Coliseum in Vancouver, Canada, on May 17, 1974. (©*Richard Pechner/rpechner.com*)

hand began cutting holes in the stage so the water would drain away. For some reason, nobody got electrocuted. Which I guess we could all thank Bear for."

After his chronic alcoholism had led to failing health and caused him to stop touring with the Grateful Dead nine months earlier, Ron "Pigpen" McKernan died, at the age of twenty-seven, after suffering a gastrointestinal hemorrhage on March 8, 1973. Although the Dead continued touring without him, Jerry Garcia returned to his bluegrass roots and joined David Grisman, Peter Rowan, Richard Greene, and John Kahn to form Old and in the Way. The band went out on tour and played eighteen club dates, all of which Bear recorded, and he is credited as one of the recording engineers on their four live albums.

As so often happened when Bear was in charge of the sound at a performance, he also became part of the show. At an Old and in the Way show at the Keystone in Berkeley in March 1973, whenever guitarist Peter Rowan and Jerry Garcia repeatedly stepped up to the microphones, the feedback was so loud that they could not begin to play.

As guitarist Peter Rowan described it, "I was standing next to Garcia when he nudged me. He said, 'Hey, man. Look up in the sound booth. Look at Owsley.' And there was Owsley in the sound booth like Lucifer. He had patch cords around his neck. He had wires in his teeth. From way down below, we could only see this maniacal grin on his bottom-lit face. Garcia said, 'He really loves his job, you know? He really loves it, man.' "

In July of that same year, the Dead fulfilled their contract with Warner Bros. Records by releasing an album entitled *History of the Grateful Dead, Volume One*, which then became more commonly known as *Bear's Choice*. Composed entirely of tracks that Bear had recorded while the band performed at Fillmore East on February 13 and 14, 1970, the album was intended as a tribute to Pigpen and was both engineered and produced by Bear. The back cover of the album also featured the first appearance of a logo that became known as "the dancing bears" (as Bear pointed out, they were actually marching) that had been designed by Bob Thomas.

Beginning in 1993, various other shows that Bear had recorded while he was on the road with the band began to be released as part of the extensive series known as *Dick's Picks*, which were initially compiled by Grateful Dead tape archivist Dick Latvala. Had it not been for Bear, the tapes would never have existed.

"I had kept a diary of my sonic mixes whenever I worked with the Dead, starting with my second or third gig with them in 1966. I was mixing the sound and I had a stereo recorder with me and I thought, 'Why not put this all on tape so I can listen to it later?' So if I had microphones attached to the mixing board and I was mixing, there was a tape. Since I was doing all that work, why just let it all go out in the air and be gone forever? And then for a while when we'd go back to the hotel after the show, we'd all be high and we'd listen to the tape. That went on for a few years, and then they got tired of it and I got tired of it as well.

"I'd say that I've never listened to ninety percent of the show tapes that I've got in my archives. No one has. I never thought of making an album out of any of them until *Dick's Picks* came along. And neither did the Dead. It was always, like, 'Oh, that's just something that Bear does. What a nuisance. What a waste of time. Why does he do that? Well, it's his machine. So, who cares?' Back then nobody cared about it but me."

Despite Bear's efforts to continue serving the Dead in every possible way, the band "kept shifting me around in the scene. They
wanted to play bigger and bigger shows, and they had to keep rent-
ing sound systems that didn't coordinate very well with their gear,
and so they asked me, 'What can we do? Do something.' I was the
guy who had started rock 'n' roll sound, and I said, 'You can build
something big, but you may not like it. It will take a lot of design
work.' But they were game and they went for it."

Bear's initial concept was to create "a single source for each instrument and each voice. Garcia's system was a single column that
had a very high gain in level like an antenna with all of the speakers stacked one on top of another so they would add and multiply
the sound without distributing much of it vertically. I wanted it to
function as a line radiator because the audience was on the ground
in front of the band.

"The entire system consisted of a cluster of line arrays that I developed and then tested in the way that line arrays work. Number
one in a line array, if it's composed of three different clusters, each
of which is a certain frequency range with a crossover, then the bass
is the longest column of speakers, the midrange is shorter, and the
highs are shorter than that. But, much like a radio transmitter, they
must all be the same radiating wavelength. Each array must be as
wide as it is tall or it doesn't work right, and you can't hang them in
isolation. I see myself as an innovator and a conceptualist. When I
work on things, I don't ever look for somebody else's solution to a
problem. I don't even think there might be one. Because I don't
care."

What came to be known as the Wall of Sound made its debut at
the Cow Palace in San Francisco on March 23, 1974. Standing forty

feet high and seventy feet wide, the system consisted of 88 fifteen-inch JBL speakers, 174 twelve-inch JBL speakers, 288 five-inch JBL speakers, and 54 Electro-Voice tweeters. In Dennis McNally's words, the array was "not merely a sound system, it was an electronic sculpture." Encased in a huge framework of metal scaffolding, it also closely resembled something that had only ever before been seen in a science fiction movie.

Driven by more than twenty-six thousand watts of power generated by fifty-five McIntosh MC-2300 amplifiers, the music that the Dead were making came through nine different channels as well as a four-way crossover network before being fed through the amplifiers and speakers into the house. In Phil Lesh's words, playing through the Wall of Sound was like "piloting a flying saucer. Or riding your own soundwave."

Financed by the Dead, the Wall of Sound had cost $350,000 to develop, the equivalent of nearly $1.8 million today. At a time when the band was trying to keep the cost of tickets low, the system required a crew of sixteen to transport and maintain. The Wall of Sound took so much time to set up that two different stages had to be purchased at an additional cost of $200,000. Four trucks were then needed to haul seventy-five tons of equipment from one gig to the next.

During the Grateful Dead's first show outdoors with the Wall of Sound at the University of Nevada in Reno on May 12, 1974, the wind started blowing so hard that the twelve-hundred-pound sound cluster above drummer Bill Kreutzmann's head began swaying back and forth. Terrified that if all the gear that was now hanging directly over him from a single winch ever came crashing down, he would be "as flat as a penny on a railroad track," Kreutzmann insisted that the crew rerig the setup before he performed beneath it again.

Aptly, Kreutzmann described the Wall of Sound as "Owsley's brain, in material form. It was his dream, but it spawned a monster that rose from the dark lagoon of his unconscious mind." In ways that Bear himself had never anticipated, the Wall of Sound was, in Kreutzmann's words, "impossible to tame."

Despite all the problems, he had achieved precisely what the Dead had asked him to do. "The Wall of Sound was a system which gave every iota of control to the musicians onstage. With a central cluster and all the monitors pulled back so everything was coming from one spot, the sound turned into something that no one had ever heard before. It was loud without being too loud. It was articulate. Every single note had a space around it. Once the system was set, I could walk away from the board because it all came from the musicians, which had been my goal right from the beginning."

Although Phil Lesh would later write that the music made by the band during the forty-odd shows they performed through the Wall of Sound are still regarded by their legion of devoted fans as the pinnacle of the Dead's live performances, the system soon proved to be completely impractical.

In Bob Weir's words, "The Wall of Sound worked just fine. It was just a logistical near impossibility. By that time, we were selling out hockey arenas, but as we went from one to another, they had to have a full crew call the day before just to set it up in time for the show. We were selling out everywhere we played, but losing money because the overhead put us in the hole. It was insane."

At a band meeting in August 1974, everyone working for the

Grateful Dead was informed that the band was going to stop touring in October. Chronically unwilling to ever fire anyone, the Dead
had finally realized that they could no longer afford to pay the outsized crew they had brought on board to install and transport the
Wall of Sound. Bear himself had "no idea how much it cost to put
the Wall of Sound together. It was huge and just what I wanted in
the beginning, but no one could sustain it and I got blamed for it
in the end."

Richard Loren, who was now the Dead's road manager, told
Jerry Garcia that the Wall of Sound was ruining the band finan-
cially. Realizing he had no other choice in the matter, Garcia reluctantly agreed that Bear's state-of-the-art sound system had to be
scrapped. For the Grateful Dead, an era had come to an end, and
it would be two years before they again performed live.

With the band that had provided him with his livelihood ever
since he had gotten out of prison no longer on the road and his career
as the world's greatest LSD street chemist now long behind him,
Bear had to find some way to earn a living. Moving to Marin County,
he began growing dope.

16

Growing Weed

Carrying flashlights and placards that read BETTER GIGS, BETTER P.A., and EGYPT OR BUST, Mickey Hart and Phil Lesh came to Bill Graham's Marin County home late one night in 1978 to ask the promoter if he would take the Grateful Dead to Egypt so they could fulfill their current fantasy by performing live before the Great Pyramids. Graham's reply was "There's a fucking war going on over there."

Refusing to take no for an answer, the band made the trip happen on their own. Accompanied by a large retinue of friends, fans, and family that included Ken Kesey, Paul Krassner, Bill Graham, and Bill Walton, who was then recovering from foot surgery as a member of the Portland Trail Blazers, the Grateful Dead performed their first show in Egypt at sundown on September 14, 1978. By then, Bear was already deeply involved in what had become his new-found avocation.

"When they quit in 1974, I had to support myself somehow, so I started growing weed. I didn't have time to go over to the warehouse in Novato every day like Dan Healy and hang out with them. When the band came together again, they didn't pick me back up. No one came out and said, 'Bear, we want to start playing together again. Do you want to come be our soundman?' like they had done after the Carousel Ballroom had ended. Even though he couldn't mix a cake from a Betty Crocker package, Dan Healy became their soundman again just like he had been back in 1967."

Phil Lesh, who had always been Bear's staunchest ally in the band, then came to his rescue by bringing him back out on the road for a couple of Grateful Dead tours as his personal roadie. Before long, Bear once again found himself at odds with the rest of the crew.

"I got into trouble because I had organized Phil's gear so completely that my stuff was always up in about ten minutes and then back down again and in the box in ten minutes. So I was out there trying to help the other guys, and that was a no-no. That was something I shouldn't have been doing. That was no good because they couldn't work with me.

"The Dead came to me just before they went to Egypt and said, 'We don't think we want you to work with us there, but we want you to go.' And I said, 'Fuck you. You want me in Egypt but you don't want me working? Get lost.' I said, 'You're going to the high temple of alchemy and the band is going to sit in the studio until a week before the first show to try to make a record? You're crazy. You should be rehearsing. You should be out on the road doing warm-up gigs. What the hell's wrong with you?' But they didn't want to hear that shit from me."

No longer able to exert control over the band in any way, Bear received a phone call the night before one of the Grateful Dead's charter flights was scheduled to depart for Cairo. Taking advantage of an offer of three free tickets, Bear flew to Egypt with two friends and spent a week exploring the pyramids before the band arrived two days before the first show. The Dead then amused themselves by smoking hashish, climbing the Great Pyramid of Giza, and riding camels in the desert.

Although Bear had already figured out how to wire the Great Pyramid to attain the best possible sound, no one wanted to listen to him. "They were trying to make the King's Chamber into an echo chamber, and I said, 'Number one, that's the wrong use for it, and number two, the chamber is the wrong dimension and sonically bad.' I wanted to use the descending passage from the Queen's Chamber as a big organ and drive it resonantly and use it as a delay system. That would have been fantastic, but they wouldn't do it. Instead, they said, 'We don't want you. Get lost.' I said, 'Okay, fine,' and I went off and did my own thing, and they kept trying to wire up the King's Chamber the wrong way."

On Saturday, September 16, 1978, the Grateful Dead performed before one of their smallest audiences since the Acid Tests. Six hundred and ninety people had paid to be there, while thousands of Bedouin on camels watched and listened for free out in the surrounding desert. The total lunar eclipse that took place during the show only added to what was already a thoroughly surreal event.

In Bear's words, "Sure enough, the big night of the last show came with a full moon, and I was onstage and the guy who was doing the sound came over to me and said they were having a lot of trouble, and I said, 'Hey, I just dropped two hundred mikes, man, and I'm not going anywhere,' and that was it."

Bear's long-running term of service with the Grateful Dead had in fact finally ended and he would never again work for the band. Finding employment with the Jefferson Starship as their onstage monitor mixer, Bear began looking for an improved monitor cabinet and went to visit John Meyer, "who was in Berkeley trying to sell a theater-system concept to Francis Coppola for *Apocalypse Now*. I was blown away by the sound of a speaker that John had built in Switzerland. It was the first speaker I had ever heard that sounded totally 'coherent,' and it was somewhat like comparing a laser to a lightbulb.

"I surprised him with my description of what it was doing, which he only knew about from his instruments but I could hear perfectly clearly. Once he realized I knew what I was going on about, I was able to coax him into abandoning his theatrical-speaker concept to concentrate on designing super-quality speakers for live music, starting with the monitors I needed for the Starship. The meeting resulted in the development of the world's finest sound-reinforcing equipment and the founding of a very successful business. As I intended, the Dead were also a beneficiary of John Meyer's excellent products."

Although Bear soon learned that this was no way to make a living, he had by then begun growing high-quality marijuana along with two partners in Fairfax just up the hill from Bolinas Road in Marin County. "I did that for about seven years from 1974 to 1981. We would get about fifteen pounds of weed from the garden. An ounce was two hundred and fifty dollars, and a pound went for somewhere between fifteen hundred and two thousand dollars if it was really good. The whole crop was about thirty thousand dollars, and I was making about ten or twelve grand a year and paying eight hundred dollars a month in rent and so always wound up in the hole.

"Basically, we worked twenty-four hours a day, seven days a week, because somebody always had to be there for four or five months. So we were working for about a dollar twenty-five an hour. It was the most dangerous, underpaid job I ever had in my life, but I did it because I loved it and I was into the breeding. I never smoked pot heavily, but I had some strains that were absolutely unbelievable. I wasn't really a grower. I was a dilettante, playing with breeding plants and growing enough of them so I could support my hobby for a few years while I was doing it because it was all so fascinating to me."

Bear might have gone right on pursuing his newfound avocation as the Luther Burbank of weed if he had not been attacked one night by some local junkies who had come to steal his crop just before it was ready to be harvested. "One of the junkies was a Vietnam vet with a stocking over his face who knew how to use a weapon, and at one point he was aiming a rifle at my chest while this black guy held a pistol up under my chin. I realized I could be dead in a second, and they said, 'Well, any unfinished business?' And I said, 'No. I've done everything I need to do. There isn't really that much I care about.'

"And then in one absolutely uninterrupted motion, I grabbed both guns and moved them away from my body in a single continuous sweep. The twenty-two fired twice just as it cleared my clothing, and then the Vietnam vet brought the butt of his rifle around and smacked me on the side of my head so hard that I went to the ground, and then he stomped me on the back of my knees in such a way that I couldn't stand up for about a day."

A friend who had come to visit that night drove up to the house just as Bear was being attacked. Dropping to the ground, the friend rolled beneath a bush and hid. Knowing someone was out there, the junkies decided not to begin ripping off the crop. Making his way to a phone, Bear called his coworkers and they phoned another friend, who promptly jumped into his car and drove up the hill.

"So here was this guy coming up the driveway as one of the junkies was trying to get away by climbing over the fence, which he didn't know was electrified. He found out about that pretty fast as he was being knocked to the ground by nine-thousand-volt pulses. Just as the other junkie was tying me up with my own garden hose, this guy came up the driveway, so off they went."

Bear then called a friend who lived farther up the hill and he arrived with a MAC-10 nine-millimeter pistol that could fire more than twelve hundred rounds a minute. "When you fired it, it just made a *pop*. Like a lightbulb breaking. We knew the junkies were still around because we could hear them talking. This son of a bitch was firing a twenty-two at us, and you'd think a Vietnam vet would have realized that he was outgunned when that nine millimeter went crashing through the bush. But, no, these guys were so determined to steal our pot that they went off a little ways, and one of my partners snuck up on them and heard them planning to come back, not the next night, but the night after that with a crew."

After fortifying the property, Bear hired some people to help him protect his crop. "We armed ourselves to the teeth, and sure enough they came. And sure enough, there was a running gun battle. There were all kinds of bullets lodged in the walls of the house, and one of the invaders got a bullet through his biceps and we drove them off.

I don't know why, but nobody called the cops. But we had to rip out all our pot and lost thousands of dollars."

Since the dope-growing community in Marin County was then still fairly small, it only took Bear a few weeks to find out who the attackers were. "But there wasn't anything I could do about it and they never came back." As fantastic as this tale seems even now, the moral of the story for Bear was "I have a rule. No matter what happens, don't panic. The more that the stress increases, the more cool and calculating I become. Like when I pulled those guns off my body. There I was, facing these guys who were obviously belligerent, armed, dangerous, and a lot bigger than me, and yet I calmly grabbed those guns and pulled them off my body. Why? Because I am not afraid of anything."

Throughout the rest of Bear's life, this was a trait that would prove to be both a blessing and a curse.

17

Bear's Dream

The first time that Grateful Dead biographer Dennis McNally ever met Bear was at a Rhythm Devils concert featuring Phil Lesh, Mickey Hart, Bill Kreutzmann, Airto Moreira, Flora Purim, and Mike Hinton at the Marin Civic Center on the weekend of February 13–14, 1981. Then thirty-one years old, McNally had already written *Desolate Angel: Jack Kerouac, the Beat Generation, and America*. Jerry Garcia had liked the book so much that he suggested McNally begin working on an authorized history of the Grateful Dead.

In McNally's words, "I was just the brand-new biographer, starting to break in and take my hazing, and that was the first time I had ever gone into a show through the backstage door. I came in early for the sound check, and Bear was mixing and everything was already late. Whether that was Bear's fault or not, I don't know, but the show itself was patently late.

"Phil Lesh was part of this, and he was not a master of patience and he was growling and fuming and glaring at Bear, who was standing at the sound board with a tablecloth that he was putting down before putting the actual board on the table. It was cloth. It was not technical. It was not the equipment. But it had to be arranged perfectly. Because this was Bear after all.

"And there was Phil Lesh trying to generate pressure, and of course Bear was impervious to all that stuff. He simply went deaf when he chose to do so, and I was thinking, 'Nothing has changed in twenty years. Nothing has changed. This is the way it has always been.' That was my first insight into Bear. He was in his own world."

On April 25, 1981, Jerry Garcia, Bob Weir, Mickey Hart, Bill Kreutzmann, and John Kahn performed a forty-minute acoustic set at the Berkeley Community Theatre as part of a benefit concert for the Seva Foundation, a charity dedicated to treating blindness all over the world founded by Wavy Gravy and Ram Dass that had initially been funded by Steve Jobs. The show also featured Country Joe McDonald, Rosalie Sorrels, Kate Wolf, and Odetta.

Although Bear had not done live sound since his time with the Jefferson Starship two years earlier, he volunteered to do the mix for the concert. Still, he was constitutionally unable to accept that this task could ever be properly done in any way but his own, and those who had accepted his offer to do the job got far more than they had bargained for that night.

"By this time, I knew you had to do all the sound through a single system, and I wanted everything set up stage right, but they said no. I said, 'What do you mean no? I'm the sound mixer.' This guy said, 'Well, it's our PA system and we won't do it. The band won't let us.' I said, 'The band has nothing to say about it.' When I had first started working with the Grateful Dead, I didn't know any better so I would stupidly delay the PA, but now I knew that it just didn't work.

"So the guy set the system up the way he wanted it that night, and when nobody was around after the sound check, I went up to the mixing table and disconnected the hot wire to stage right. The show started and I turned on the system, and I had everything coming through the speakers that were stage left. I only had half the cluster, but that was all I really needed.

"The guy came up to me and said, 'Stage right is not working. We have to do something about it.' I said, 'Don't you dare touch anything. The show is on right now. I'll deal with it. You touch anything and I'll knock your block off,' and the whole night went beautifully. I had the best sound I'd ever gotten in Berkeley Community Theatre, which is a rotten hall to begin with where the sound was always lousy.

"At the end of the night while everyone was relaxing, I opened up this little connector and soldered the wires back on and put it all back together. This same guy came back up to me and said he had to find out what had been wrong with the system. I turned it on for him and it worked perfectly. He said, 'What's going on here?' And I said, 'Hey, don't worry about it. These sort of things happen all the time.' The guy kept apologizing for what he thought was a screwup, but it was just what I wanted.

"In every way, what happened that night was just so typical of what still goes on in the sound business today. It's full of egos and people who only know that you have to hang line arrays. I know more about line arrays than anybody, including John Meyer, and I know you cannot use a line array by itself. Two strings of speakers, one hanging down on each side of the stage, sound like dog shit. No matter how hard you try, you simply cannot ever make them sound right."

Eleven months later, on March 20, 1982, Bear took some acid with friends on the day of the vernal equinox. After going to bed that night, Bear had a dream in which he saw the planet "as if I was out on a satellite and the whole northern half of the earth was all wrapped up in this swirling cloud, and I realized I was watching something like the Deluge in the Bible."

When Bear awoke the next morning, he told his housemate Bob Thomas about this "weird dream I'd had. I said I had never seen anything like it before, and we both marveled at it, and then I stopped thinking about it and went on with my day. My opinion had always been that dreams are things you entertain yourself with at night, but when I woke up the next morning, I realized I'd had the exact same dream again, and I couldn't ever remember having had the same dream twice."

When Bear returned home later that day, Bob Thomas told him that he had heard about someone on the radio who had just given a lecture about carbon dioxide and the ice age cycle. "I said, 'Oh, well. That's very interesting. I wonder who that is.' And then I went to bed that night, and the next morning just before I woke up, I had this same dream again. Third time in a row, and by then, boy, I was freaked."

Bear then began looking for any kind of clues he could find that might help explain the mystery of his recurring dream. After calling around, Bear found a professor at Berkeley who told him that if he really wanted to learn about this subject, he should contact George Kukla.

Born in Czechoslovakia, Kukla had gone to Columbia University on an exchange program in 1971 and then become a senior research scientist at the university's Lamont-Doherty Earth Observatory. In 1972, Kukla and geologist Robert Matthews of Brown University had convened a historic conference on glacial cooling and what they feared was the advent of another ice age. After their findings had been published in *Science* magazine, the Nixon administration established a panel to investigate the matter.

Over the phone, Kukla told Bear that he would soon be attending a meeting in La Jolla and urged Bear to call him again there. "Then I went to sleep and I had that same dream again for the fourth time. So I called him down in La Jolla, and I was telling him about the dream, and all of a sudden the line went dead. And I went, 'Oh, fuck. This is so weird. I better go down and see him.' So I jumped on a plane and went down there and met him and talked to him about the ice age cycle."

Slipping into the back row at the meeting, Bear began listening to a lecture about the blocking effects of high-pressure ridges only to realize that he was attending a meeting of meteorologists sponsored by the National Oceanic and Atmospheric Association, also known as NOAA. In Bear's somewhat fevered state of mind, the synchronicity was so overwhelming that even the acronym seemed to be part of the grand design. "*Noaa* is a word that doesn't exist in either ancient Egyptian or Hebrew. So I began thinking that Noah really does exist but that it referred to this atmospheric association."

As the lecturer explained that the computer model used to predict weather was no longer working because a high-pressure ridge had appeared in a place where it was not normally found and the low-pressure area was being amplified because of it, Bear began thinking about an article he had read in *Scientific American* about a vortex tube that could separate hot and cold and seemed to him like a practical demonstration of Maxwell's demon.

After returning home from the conference, Bear went right on having the same dream night after night. Although he was clearly being sent a message, he could not understand what it meant. "I got to the point where I couldn't even drink a glass of wine with meals. I mean, talk about my drug tolerance being zero. I thought I was losing my nut. After about three weeks, the dream finally stopped when I figured out that the event I was dreaming about was thermodynamic in nature and located in the shadow of winter in Baffin Bay, which is a *polynya*, or a permanently unfrozen area of water, near Greenland in the arctic circle."

Plunging into research on the subject much as he had done while teaching himself how to make LSD in the Bancroft Library in Berkeley, Bear discovered that atmospheric energy in that region began rising dramatically every year around the middle of December and then fell off again in February when the sun began to shine on Baffin Bay. Consisting of roughly forty days and nights, Bear reckoned this was the period during which the Great Deluge described in the Bible had taken place.

Using Egyptian chronology, Bear then learned that the seventeenth day of their second month was celebrated as the festival of the goddess Hathor, the bringer of the yearly flood of the Nile that enabled the Egyptians to grow their crops. "When you compute the seventeenth day of the second month, putting the flood of Noah on the festival day of Hathor is very interesting because that is about the sixteenth to the twentieth of December. Which is why the Christians put the birth of Christ at the time of this festival. Why do people celebrate the winter solstice? Because if they made it through to the solstice and there had been no storm, they knew it wasn't going to happen until the following year."

With the energy level in the atmosphere rising dramatically each year, Bear believed that the trigger point for the next Great Deluge was near. "When this storm happens, which I call an ultra-cyclone, the rains come, the winds blow everything flat, there are waves a thousand feet tall, and the earth appears to be covered in water. Although the storm only lasts for forty days, it removes so much heat from the earth that it takes a hundred thousand years of ice building to replace it.

"All the northern cities are getting hotter. The weather is getting more intense. Rainstorms are getting huge. There are floods and cyclones and hurricanes like never before. And the polar ice cap is melting at a dramatic rate, raising the sea level to a point where the big storm happens. During the storm, the seas will rise three hundred feet. And when they do, so far as all the people who live in the northern hemisphere are concerned, their days are numbered. I don't see how anyone there could survive it."

Despite how far-fetched Bear's notions about the coming ice age seemed to many of those who knew him, John Perry Barlow found himself "on an airplane one day with Stephen Schneider, who was then the leading theorist in how to model large-scale global change. After we had established who we were, I said, 'You aren't by any chance familiar with the beliefs of my old friend Owsley, are you?' And he said, 'Oh my God, I'm much more familiar with those beliefs than I wish I were.' And I said, 'Well, what do you think?' And he said, 'Well, he's onto something. But he says it in a way I find so disagreeable.'"

Possessed by his apocalyptic vision of an ice age storm that would destroy the northern half of the planet, Bear went to Australia for the first time in 1982. Unable to stay there for more than three months because he had entered the country on a tourist visa, Bear would regularly return to Australia during the next two years.

In 1984, Bear appeared at Phil Lesh's house with a map of the world showing the mean temperatures at the height of the last ice age and delivered what David Gans described as "a ninety minute lecture on a thermal cataclysm that he said would begin with a six-week rainstorm and leave the entire Northern Hemisphere uninhabitable." Bear then passed out Australian visa applications to all those who were present.

By selling off much of what he owned, Bear raised enough money to take others, his daughter Redbird and her mother, Melissa Cargill, among them, along with him to Australia. Like one of the pioneers who had settled the Old West, Bear then began making a brand-new life for himself in the land down under.

18

The Land Down Under

~~~

Located about nine miles from the town of Atherton in Queensland in the northeast corner of Australia, the 126 acres of rocky hillside studded with eucalyptus trees on which Bear would live for the rest of his life could only be reached by driving down a five-mile dirt track that often became impassable during the winter rains. Bear claimed the property, which sloped down to the Walsh River at an elevation of three thousand feet, by squatting on it.

By the time the local authorities discovered him there in 1986, Bear had already built a few sheds and installed "a reticulated water system, a septic system, and a nine-kilowatt generator to provide electricity. I had also planted some gardens where I was growing what I thought was some of the finest-flavored coffee in the world. When they found out I was living here, they said, 'You don't have the right to do that.' And I said, 'Well, but look what I've done.'"

Not about to give up the land without a fight, Bear then pleaded

Bear onstage at Laughter, Love, and Music, the memorial concert for Bill Graham in Golden Gate Park on November 4, 1991. *(Ed Perlstein/Getty Images)*

his case in person before the minister of Queensland. "I told him we had taken very good care of the property and protected the native plants and trees, and then I said, 'Besides, I understand there is a tradition of squatting in this area.' They didn't want to hear about that because every squatter from the time of the first fleet that ever came to Australia has had to fight tooth and nail to get tenure. They still called it Crown property even though there was no lease or freehold or any claims on it. It was just open primeval forest on the river."

Eventually, Bear was granted a permit to occupy five acres of the property, which he felt was not nearly enough to keep other people from moving in around him. The authorities then offered him twenty-six acres of land. "I said, 'That's a fourth of what we had planned. We have two families living here.' Finally, I gave up arguing with them and hired a crew and fenced the whole thing. About a year later, they came back and said, 'Gee, you're not supposed to do that.' The fence was like nine-tenths of possession because when you get a lease here, you are required to fence the property within a year or the lease will lapse."

After having finally secured a ninety-nine-year lease on the land, Bear began constructing a complex of buildings, sheds, modified shipping containers, and caravans that Bob Weir called "a sort of a science fiction version of the way that hippies used to live in America in the seventies."

In addition to his original generator, Bear had by then acquired a portable range generator and a diesel generator as well. He had also installed two solar-energy systems as well as a wind generator mounted on a hundred-foot tower that reliably provided him with fifteen hundred watts of power. Bear described the nine-foot-high, two-hundred-square-foot hexagonal tent with a raised wooden floor in which he slept as "looking like something out of *The Arabian Nights.*"

Through a gutter and a drainpipe that he had mounted on the roof of an unfinished cottage, rainwater flowed through a strainer into a fifteen-hundred-gallon tank that supplied all of his drinking water. Another three-thousand-gallon tank provided the cooling bath for one of his generators. Bear also installed two more septic systems on the property, thereby enabling him to enjoy a bath, a shower, or a session in his hot tub after one of his regular weight-lifting workouts in his gym. The property also featured three fully rigged kitchens as well as a variety of tents in which his guests stayed.

In John Perry Barlow's words, "He was living goddamn close to nowhere. I drove a long ways out there in my rented car before I came upon it, and I didn't see any other sign of human habitation. Melissa Cargill lived nearby, and I believe everybody on the property had at one time either been married to Bear or heavily affiliated with him.

"I didn't stay with him, and I'm kind of sorry I didn't because it was like something out of *Lord Jim*. Sheds and pavilions in the jungle, but the main living area was rather Victorian, handsomely carpeted with lots of books and nice furniture and no walls. It was quite plush. He had stuff you hadn't even thought of, and with Bear, wind was always in ready supply."

A reasonable question would be how could Bear afford to purchase all this equipment while residing in a country where he could not earn a living because he was not yet a permanent resident. An eager and enthusiastic consumer who had always bought whatever struck his fancy, Bear's last stint of regular employment in America had been as an the onstage monitor mixer for the Jefferson

Starship in 1979. Even as a self-described "dilettante" growing weed in Marin County, Bear had barely made enough money to survive, much less be able to take others with him when he decamped to Australia for the first time in 1982.

Although there is no knowing precisely how Bear paid for all the improvements on his property, he had sold just about everything he owned before leaving California for Australia. Along with all the jewelry that he was then making, Bear might also have sold some LSD that he had made years earlier and then stashed away in places known only to him. Royalties from the albums *Bear's Choice* and *Steal Your Face* would also have enabled him to keep his head above water during this period. And as John Perry Barlow would later say, "The way Bear was living in Australia was actually not nearly as luxurious as it might have seemed to someone who never visited him there."

Whatever the true nature of his finances might have been, Bear soon began devoting most of his time to creating bronze and silver belt buckles bearing the Steal Your Face logo, which he would then bring with him to sell at Grateful Dead shows on his regular trips back to America.

"I always came back to America for the Dead tours, and I would usually go to two a year and flog my art. I'd fly to the town, rent a car and a hotel room, go to the show, and carry my stuff around. I made an arrangement with Greenpeace to have some of it displayed out in the audience. The first belt buckles were not handmade but foundry cast. I sold only a few backstage, and the best location for me by far was always in the hallways of the venue. It was a lot of work and very tiring to travel so much, but it was rewarding because I also got to hang out with my friends and hear lots of music."

By now, the band was playing massive stadium shows that were attended by a brand-new generation of Deadheads for whom Bear was a certified legend. Realizing he could make far more money by increasing the original price of his belt buckles, Bear began selling them as pieces of collectible art. As always where Bear and the Grateful Dead were concerned, his steadfast refusal to obey what had now become the rules of the road for the band continued to get him into trouble.

During the Grateful Dead's 1993 summer tour, Bear pulled his rental car up to the band's catering truck outside Soldier Field in Chicago and then blithely ordered food as though he were still a member of the crew. In the big-bucks world of the rock business in the 1990s where every dollar mattered, this was a definite no-no. But because this was Bear, whom no one had ever been able to control, he got away with it.

While Bear was in Chicago, all of his jewelry was stolen by someone who then tried to sell it to a Deadhead shop in the city. After taking it away from the thief, the people at the store tracked Bear down and offered to bring the jewelry to him at a show a week later in Washington, DC. As a Grateful Dead staffer would later say, "He was selling very beautiful necklaces that were insanely overpriced and belt buckles that cost a hundred dollars. These people had just spent hundreds of dollars on plane tickets to get there, and he looked them in the eye and said, 'Well, I obviously don't have any money. Here's a belt buckle. How about we call it square?' They were delighted and I wanted to throttle him."

Before the Dead performed at RFK Stadium in the nation's capital on June 26, 1993, Chelsea Clinton, who was then thirteen years old, came backstage with two of her friends. While anyone else might have been hesitant to even talk to the daughter of the president of the United States, Bear promptly decided to put the opportunity to good use. Striding right up to her, Bear began showing Chelsea Clinton a tray of his jewelry as though he were about to shove it up her nose.

In the words of the Grateful Dead staffer, "He had the sales tactics of a Mumbai street peddler." As the staffer stood there watching in horror, a White House employee who had accompanied Chelsea Clinton to the gig came up and said, "I don't like that." Having already learned how to deal with any stranger as a potential voter, Chelsea Clinton was trying to be as polite as possible with Bear. The same could not be said for the Secret Service agents surrounding her, who were by now most definitely alarmed and about to spring into action.

Hoping to avoid an incident that would receive extensive press coverage, the Grateful Dead staffer walked over and said, "Hey, Bear, can I talk to you for a second? Because you are about to be picked up and walked out of here." After leading Bear to a quiet corner of the room, the staffer said, "You're not going to like what I'm going to say, but I'm only trying to protect your ass. You're really coming on strong here. Would you go a little softer, please?" Without a word, Bear simply turned and walked away.

Running into a dressing room where Bob Weir and Jerry Garcia were talking to each other, the freaked-out staffer said, "'Bobby, you have to save Chelsea Clinton from Bear. I want to bring her and her friends in here. Bobby said, 'Sure, why not? Let's talk to Chelsea.' So I brought Chelsea and her friends into the innermost sanctum, where there was no one else but them and Jerry and Bobby."

The next day, Bear grabbed the staffer by the arm. Enraged,

the staffer said, "Get your fucking hands off me. I'm listening to you." Bear then said, "You don't respect my art, do you?" The staffer replied, "I respect your art a lot. I don't like your manners." Bear said, "See this laminate? This gives me the right to do what I want."

"No, it doesn't," the staffer told him. "It doesn't give you the right to impose on our guests or abuse them. And I don't know where you got the idea that you could make a living off the fucking Grateful Dead by selling jewelry backstage." Although Bear then went to Phil Lesh to complain about the way in which he had been treated, his plea fell on deaf ears.

Having already embraced the Internet as the perfect means by which to communicate with all those who were still fascinated by him without ever having to meet them in person, Bear also began selling his jewelry on www.thebear.org. The Web site also featured essays he had written about the true nature of psychedelics; the real reasons for drug prohibition as well as how the drug laws needed to be rewritten; the coming ice age; his belief that global warming as well as the greenhouse effect were utter nonsense; his assessment of the faults and virtues of analog versus digital recording; the delete-rious effect of shows such as *Sesame Street* on children's ability to learn how to read; and the role that diet and exercise had played in his life.

Noting that after his teenage years, his weight had suddenly bal-looned from 125 to 168 pounds in just six months, Bear informed the world that he had then gone on a restricted-calorie diet that had enabled him to lose twenty-six pounds. After taking up ballet, Bear had adopted the high-fat, low-carbohydrate diet that he then fol-lowed for the rest of his life.

Long before anyone had ever heard of the diet of meat, nuts, and berries that hunter-gatherers had consumed during the Paleolithic period, Bear compared his all-meat regimen to what the Eskimos had always eaten without having suffered any deficiencies in their health. Feeling he was losing strength and not at all pleased by the way he looked, Bear noted that he had started lifting weights again in 1990 at the age of fifty-five just as he had done back when he was in prison.

Getting into it as only he could, Bear had begun working out with heavy weights for an hour, then giving himself two days to recover before his next session. By doing so, he thus added nearly thirty pounds of muscle over the next seven years. An avid reader of bodybuilding magazines, Bear had done his best to emulate the Heavy Duty lifting program espoused by Mike Mentzer, who had been named Mr. Olympia in the heavyweight class in 1979.

Although Bear was working out as hard as he possibly could to clear his head while also keeping himself in top physical shape, he was quick to dismiss Arnold Schwarzenegger's well-known comment that getting a pump from lifting weights was much like an orgasm. "I've had a lot of heavy pumps," Bear said. "And none of them was even remotely like an orgasm."

Despite his occasional travails on the road with the Grateful Dead, Bear had now set himself up for life in a country where he was not only safe from the coming ice-age storm but also felt very much at home. Comfortably ensconced in the enclave he had created from scratch in an ancient rain forest in Australia, Bear had everything but someone to share it all with him.

19

Real Love

~~~

On July 13, 1984, as the Grateful Dead performed "Dark Star" for the first time in three years beneath a full moon at the Greek Theatre in Berkeley, Bear met the woman with whom he would spend the rest of his life. Then thirty-two years old, Sheilah Manning had been working in the Grateful Dead ticket office for a couple of years while also teaching children's dance classes in Marin County and helping to run a cooperative secondhand clothing business in Sausalito.

Born in Wellesley, Massachusetts, she had attended Vermont College before going off to join her boyfriend at Tufts University. By then, they had already taken acid together, and he had turned her on to *The Electric Kool-Aid Acid Test*. High on LSD, Sheilah Manning saw the Grateful Dead for the first time in Boston in 1973 and was immediately entranced by Jerry Garcia. "He was very impressive. I was mesmerized by his talent. Having spent time around guitar players, I recognized his immense talent right away. What he played was light, beautifully lyrical, and tasteful, very intricate yet looked effortless. I planted myself in front of Jerry and watched in awe."

Dropping out of school, she accompanied her boyfriend to California. After they split up, she lived in Mill Valley for a while and then began seeing Spencer Dryden, a fabled character who while serving as the drummer in the Jefferson Airplane had been Grace Slick's boyfriend. Along with bassist Jack Casady, who had been Melissa Cargill's lover, Dryden had helped provide the bottom for the band's driving, soaring sound.

"Spencer Dryden came from the LA scene," Jerry Garcia would later say. "It's like a whole 'nother trip down there. It's that thing of, 'Look out for the sharpies, man. . . .' Down there, they've got that ultra-paranoia, especially if there's money involved. Spencer was like a model of one of those guys who go, 'They're going to *burn* you. Those fuckers will burn you *every* time.' Which of course they then *always* do. You know?"

The nephew of Charlie Chaplin, Dryden had left the Jefferson Airplane after watching Marty Balin get punched out by a Hells Angel at Altamont. When Sheilah Manning met him, Dryden was the drummer in the New Riders of the Purple Sage, a band that he also later managed. Quite a bit older than her at the time, he "seemed very kind and caring. We had a brief relationship when he was on the road, but it quickly dissolved when I realized he was actually living with someone in California."

While shopping at the Marin City flea market one day, Sheilah Manning "came upon a woman who was selling a bunch of various things including clothing that looked very familiar to me. I felt like

I knew the person who had worn these clothes. The woman explained that she was selling her ex-boyfriend's belongings to get some money together to move out because their relationship was over. After chatting with her for a while longer, I realized the ex-boyfriend to whom she was referring was Spencer.

"We stayed in touch for a while after that, and a few weeks later she called me to say that she was going for a job at the Grateful Dead ticket office in San Rafael that Spencer had arranged for her. She then called me to say that she had not taken the job because she smoked cigarettes and the office was smoke-free and suggested I try for the job. I went to the Dead office in San Rafael and was offered the job right away."

When Bear walked by Sheilah Manning at the show at the Greek Theatre, she already knew who he was. After someone introduced them, they began talking. Moving quickly, as he always did when he was attracted to a woman, Bear invited her to attend a wedding with him in Sonoma County. After they had gone out to dinner together, Bear asked her if she wanted to visit him in Australia. Her response was "Not particularly."

After assuring her that property now in fact had a toilet, Bear then sent Sheilah a round-trip ticket. "In Australia, I took acid with him fairly quickly. We were sharing a shed with another couple, and I stayed with Bear for a couple of months before heading back to California. I liked being there, but it was so different from what I was used to that I wasn't sure I wanted to live there. I did really like being with Bear though. We enjoyed one another's company, and I missed him when I went back to California."

For the next four years, Bear and Sheilah Manning continued to see each other in Australia as well as whenever he would come to

America to sell his wares on Grateful Dead tours. "Bear came back to the United States for a while, and then we went back to Australia together. Because we only had tourist visas, we had to leave the country every six months and come back to America. I still wasn't sure I wanted to move permanently to Australia, but what was clear to both of us from my first visit on was that we wanted to be together.

"On one of our trips back to the United States, the Australian authorities noticed that we had been regularly going in and out of Australia for the past few years. As this was against regulations, they permanently canceled our tourist visas right then and there and told us that we would not be able to return until we had applied for residential status from outside of the country. For the next two years, we rented a house in Marin County while Bear applied for residential status as a 'distinguished artist.'"

Since one of the primary criteria for the visa was that the applicant had to have been internationally recognized for outstanding achievements in the arts, Bear began obtaining what eventually amounted to thirty letters of support attesting to his artistic skills from people like Jackson Browne, Bill Graham, and Bob Weir.

The testimonial that probably did Bear the most good came from a most unlikely source. Having purchased a gold crocodile medallion as well as several other pieces of jewelry from Bear while touring America with the Rolling Stones, lead guitarist Keith Richards sent the Australian authorities a handwritten letter verifying that Bear was in fact an artist of international repute. Not surprisingly, he was granted official permission to reside permanently in Australia.

Sheilah, who had been looking after Phil and Jill Lesh's children while Bear once again began growing weed in Marin County, finally decided to migrate with him to Australia. After they had both moved back to the property, Bear set about re-creating the kind of scene that no one had experienced since the long-lost days of the Acid Tests by throwing a gala party that soon became a local tradition.

Once a year by invitation only on the last Saturday in Capricorn (anywhere from December 22 to January 21), musicians from as far away as Brisbane and Sydney would come to Bear's property to play continuously from eight thirty at night until four thirty in the morning for as many as a hundred people, all of whom were tripping on their host's best-known product.

"The party itself was always absolutely awesome," Bear recalled. "We never had anything that good back in the sixties and seventies. It was actually a lot more magical than almost all of the Dead shows between 1964 and 1980, and yet it was just a party in the bush. I always held it on Saturday night because that was the Acid Test night.

"I'd turn my gym into a performance area with a complete PA mounted in the trusses including monitors and a perfectly adjusted central cluster. I had microphones that cost two or three thousand dollars each, and you could go hundreds of meters from that building and the music would still sound clean and separate and perfect."

Just as he had so often done while setting up the Grateful Dead's equipment onstage before a show, Bear could still get so fixated on a task that he would become completely oblivious to everything else that was going on around him. As Sheilah would later say, "Redbird was getting married in a beautiful private resort and Bear wanted to do the sound for her wedding, and of course it had to be perfect. He brought all the speakers with him and the setup took him much longer than he thought it would.

"He was so hung up on trying to get it all exactly right that he was missing out on the party. Starfinder and I finally had to take him aside and remind him, *'Bear, your daughter is getting married here. Stop adjusting the gear!'* He then managed to relax and enjoy the reception."

On August 9, 1995, a month after the Grateful Dead had performed at Soldier Field in Chicago and eight days after his fifty-third birthday, Jerry Garcia died in a rehab facility in Forest Knolls in Marin County. Burdened by a heroin habit he could not kick, Garcia had been in poor health for years. The official cause of his death was listed as coronary artery disease that had been worsened by diabetes.

Although right from the start Bear's closest relationship within the Dead was with Phil Lesh, Jerry Garcia had always been the brilliant sun around which all the other planets in the Grateful Dead universe revolved. A Buddha-like figure who seemed to radiate his own special kind of light while also viewing the world around him with a distinct sense of wry amusement, Garcia's personal life had always been chaotic. Through the power of his music as well as his personality, he had always been able to draw others into his orbit both onstage and off.

After people had called Bear in Australia to tell him that Garcia had died, Bear began reflecting on a relationship that had begun nearly thirty years earlier at the Muir Beach Acid Test on December 18, 1965. "What happened to Garcia started in 1975 or 1976. Someone gave him what he was told was opium to smoke and it wasn't. It was ninety-five percent pure heroin base. So-called Persian. The thing about heroin when it's smoked is that the material condenses in the lungs as a tar, but it's soluble and the body slowly absorbs it so it's like sticking a needle in your vein with a drip. A constant supply.

"I had conversations with him when he was off the stuff and he said, 'Well, I really like what it does.' And I said, 'From the outside, you're not a very interesting guy to be around when you're using. You're really unpleasant.' He said, 'Well, maybe so, but I like what it does.' When he was using, his music was shit. He lost the jam and the jazz and just played the same old nonsense over and over again and it had no soul. He was like a machine. Like a tape of Garcia.

"I told him that whenever we saw one another but when he was using, he wouldn't even talk to me. When he saw me coming, he would go the other way. He would turn in the hall and say, 'I'm busy. Don't come in here now.' Or he would have someone bar his dressing-room door. When he was straight, his eyes would light up whenever he saw me and he would call me in to come sit down to talk.

"Back when we were all living in that house in LA and then later when the Dead were at 710 Ashbury, there were occasions when I would come across a little notebook Jerry had that was full of doodles. He would sit down and draw a whole page, these beautiful pen-and-ink figures of all the things he would see when he got high on acid. Beautifully detailed interlocking motifs that faded in and out of each other. Exquisite, like the finest artwork you ever saw. When most people come back down from a trip, they can't draw what they had seen anymore. But he could. He could draw it all perfectly.

"I really loved the guy. He was a remarkable individual and he was very important to me in a lot of different ways that are difficult to describe. He wasn't a godlike figure to me. He was an infinitely curious, infinitely intelligent, infinitely creative brother and in lots of ways an inspiration. When I heard about his death, I wasn't too terribly surprised at first. It didn't really hit me as a heavy loss until later in the day when Sheilah put on 'Stella Blue.' That blew out all the stops and I had a good cry."

Three months later, Bear and Sheilah Manning were married at Carrington Gardens in Atherton. A hundred people, Bear's daughter Redbird among them, attended the ceremony. Many years later, Bear would say, "Sheilah is the most important thing that ever happened to me. We are truly soul mates. We have been in love together ever since we first met, and our love is as strong today as it was in the beginning. How many people can say that?" As always with Bear, the question itself contained the answer.

20

Old and in the Way

In May 2000, Bear got his first taste of his own mortality when a doctor informed him that he had "a blockage in the main artery feeding the lower part of my heart that dated from my teenage years but had never progressed. Even when I was in my twenties and studying ballet, I'd suffered terribly from angina without ever knowing what it was. I thought it was just tired muscles in my chest. Because of this gnarly blood vessel that had twisted around itself, I had a blockage of ninety percent."

After seeking out "the best surgeon in Australia, the guy who taught this technique," Bear went to Sydney to undergo double-bypass surgery. "They did an off-pump operation using my mammary artery, and they didn't have to stop my heart. Because of my workout routine and my all-meat diet, I had such a well-developed athletic heart that the operation was beautifully successful. Both my endurance and fitness improved after the procedure, and I could still jump on a bicycle and beat Sheilah to the top of the hill."

While someone else might have thought twice about continuing to take LSD at this point in life, Bear was not about to change his ways. "I now try to do it at least once a year. Maybe twice. Because I worry about losing access. I'd love to take it more often, but it takes me like three or four days to recover from it when I do, and my days are really full."

On May 21, 2002, the Other Ones, a band composed of Bob Weir, Phil Lesh, Mickey Hart, and Bill Kreutzmann, joined by Jimmy Herring on guitar, Jeff Chimenti on keyboards, and Rob Barraco on keyboards and vocals, performed at the Alpine Valley Music Theatre in East Troy, Wisconsin. In John Perry Barlow's words, "Bear would store LSD in odd places. He hid some in a tree stump in Marin County that he dug up years later and recrystallized, and it worked in a really raw way.

"When the Dead had that supposed reunion concert at Alpine Valley, Mountain Girl and I were there, and Bear gave us some of this ancient acid and it was really gnarly. We had kind of forgotten what the real stuff was like. There was a certain point where Mountain Girl and I looked at one another and went, 'Holy shit! Fuck! Bear has messed with us.' We'd seen him take the same amount, and pretty soon we found him and he said, 'Yeah, this stuff is a little rough.'"

Despite how completely dysfunctional they could so often be, the Grateful Dead in all their various incarnations had for years been the only real family that Bear had ever known. As he grew older and his time with the band on the road decreased, his son Starfinder and his daughter Redbird began to play a far more important role in his life than they ever had before. Which was not to say that he had ever been a conventional parent to any of his children.

Although Bear had never lived for long with either of his two ex-wives, he had reached out to his son Peter when the boy was a teenager and brought him to California, where they had lived together for a while. After having located his sixteen-year-old daughter Nina, Bear called to inform her that he was her real father. While his contact with both of them remained fairly limited, the same could not be said for Bear's relationship with his son Starfinder and his daughter Redbird.

Because their mothers had such wildly differing personalities, Bear always found it far easier to deal with Melissa Cargill than Rhoney Gissen. In her memoir *Owsley and Me: My LSD Family*, co-written with Tom Davis and published in 2012, Gissen paints what can only be described as a none-too-flattering portrait of Bear while noting, "It was hard for us to agree about anything. Neither of us was agreeable by nature."

Although they were never married, Gissen had legally changed her last name to Stanley when she had entered dental school in New York City. Despite having never taken Bear to court for child support, Gissen Stanley did want her son to have an ongoing relationship with his father and so would send Starfinder to stay with Bear each summer while he was still living in California. Not surprisingly, the consequences of these annual visits were often not what she had expected.

After Starfinder's plane had landed in San Francisco one summer, Gissen Stanley was called by someone from the airlines, who informed her that no one had come to the airport to pick up her young son. Knowing Bear, she explained that he would be there at some point. Late as always, Bear finally appeared.

During another visit, Gissen Stanley called Bear and asked to speak to their son, only to have him tell her that he had sent Starfinder to Wavy Gravy's Camp Winnarainbow in Laytonville, a two-and-half-hour drive from Marin County. Having sent Starfinder to be with his father, Gissen Stanley was furious, but she then learned that the boy was having the time of his life learning how to juggle and walk on a tightrope while also taking guitar lessons at the camp. One summer, Gissen Stanley called Bear only to learn that he and Starfinder were out on the road with the Grateful Dead at the Red Rocks Amphitheatre in Colorado.

Gissen Stanley and Starfinder would also see Bear whenever he came to New York City. In the fall of 1982, Starfinder, who was then twelve years old, had just begun going to a new school, where he was being given so much homework that he could not stay out late at night. For this reason, Gissen Stanley arranged for them to meet Bear in the late afternoon at Gallaghers Steakhouse on West Fifty-Second Street in Manhattan.

After sitting down at a small table near the bar, in a restaurant that was then still empty, the two of them waited patiently for Bear to arrive. Starfinder passed the time by drawing on a sketch pad, while his mother immersed herself in a book. Over the phone earlier in the day, she had "already read Bear the riot act" by saying, "If you're late, I won't wait. If you want to see your kid, be on time." Bear's completely inappropriate response to her was "If you have to wait for me, the fact that you have a kid will make you more attractive."

Arriving only fifteen minutes late, which for him was a small miracle, Bear appeared wearing a pair of tight jeans, Tony Lama boots, "and a white T-shirt a size too small for his bulging pecs." He was also accompanied by a skinny girl, who said she was an artist from New Orleans. When Bear saw the drawing that Starfinder was sketching, he complimented his son and began looking at all the other work he had done on the pad.

From his aluminum briefcase, Bear took out a lined velvet jeweler's case, which he opened and placed on the table. Handing Gissen Stanley a jeweler's loupe so she could examine the pieces of jewelry in the case in detail, Bear showed her "a Pegasus enameled in white with tiny rubies in the wings." After Gissen Stanley told him that she loved the piece, Bear quoted her what he called "the family price" of $10,000. When Gissen Stanley expressed shock that he actually wanted her to buy the Pegasus, Bear's blithe reply was "You're a dentist. You can afford it."

As soon as the blood-rare steak that Bear had ordered for dinner appeared, he began eating it without waiting for his girlfriend to be served. Informing Gissen Stanley and Starfinder that he was planning to leave for Australia in a month, Bear asked them both to come with him. If they did, Bear promised to help teach his son how to further his obvious artistic talent. Feeling threatened by his proposal, Gissen told him that she would think about it. A month later, Bear and his girlfriend left for Australia without either Gissen Stanley or Starfinder.

In 1985, when he was fifteen years old, Starfinder ran away from home. After Gissen Stanley had spent a frantic week not knowing where her son had gone while having terrible nightmares about him in the worst situations imaginable, Starfinder called to say that his father had sent him an airplane ticket to California. The two of them were now living together in the Panama Hotel in San Rafael while Bear waited for his return visa to Australia to be renewed.

After having boarded the next plane to San Francisco, Gissen Stanley burst into tears when she saw her son. To her, the boy looked ill. His neck was swollen and he could barely speak above a whisper. The next day, Starfinder returned with his mother to New York, where a pediatrician diagnosed him as suffering from severe mononucleosis. Rather than filling the doctor's prescription for steroids to treat the illness, Gissen Stanley followed Bear's advice and fed her son calves' liver cooked rare.

After having kept her son in bed for five days, she drove Starfinder to school so he could take the PSAT. She then put him back to bed and fed him yet more liver. A week later, he was fully recovered. When Gissen Stanley learned that her son had achieved "a perfect score" on the test, she was elated. Starfinder then graduated from the University of Pennsylvania School of Veterinary Medicine and began working as a veterinarian.

Shortly after having celebrated his seventy-second birthday, Bear portrayed his role as a father: "Both Starfinder and Redbird are now exactly half my age. He is three weeks older than her, and their mothers Rhoney and Melissa are still good friends and raised them as brother and sister. I participated as much as I could. In the end, it all worked out fine for them, but it was never easy for any of us.

"Although Starfinder's genetic makeup is as different as possible from mine, he looks, sounds, and thinks more like me than any of my other children. He is so much like me that it's scary. I now also have grandchildren, and I just became a great-grandfather, so I guess I really am getting old after all."

In 2004, while Starfinder and his mother were visiting Bear in Australia, he took his son's hand and placed it on the left side of his neck so Starfinder could feel the lump that had appeared several months earlier just below Bear's jaw. Assuming that it was just an inflammation caused by a persistent toothache, Bear had gone to a dentist, who extracted the tooth and then placed Bear on a course of antibiotics that had done nothing to reduce the swelling.

A week after he had been examined by a local ear, nose, and throat doctor, Bear went to Cairns for a biopsy, which revealed that the lump bulging out of a muscle on the side of his neck was "stage four squamous-cell carcinoma that had started in my tonsils. I smoked tobacco from the age of eleven to thirteen and then quit, but I had spent years in smoky bars and venues and limousines and been backstage with people like Jerry Garcia who smoked like chimneys, and so I had been exposed to lots and lots of secondhand smoke.

"The smoke that comes off the end of a cigarette doesn't go through a filter or anybody's lungs. You just breathe it in, and secondary smoke is four times as carcinogenic as what goes through a nonfilter cigarette like a Camel, and that's where I think the cancer came from."

That his all-meat diet might also have contributed to the condition never occurred to Bear. "Normally within six months or a year of this cancer appearing, it has metastasized throughout your body. It is one of the most aggressive cancers you can get. I'd had it for at least three years, but it had grown very slowly and never left the left side of my neck. The reason for this was that I am a total carnivore. I don't eat carbohydrates. The glucose turnover in my blood is very,

very small, and cancers grow on glucose. In other words, this cancer was living in a desert.

"There is also something conscious about cancers. They grow their own nerves and blood vessels. They are completely painless until they are hit with some light radiation. Within ten minutes of my getting my first dose of radiation, I was in the most exquisite pain I'd ever experienced in my life. I was popping painkillers like they were going out of style. I had to sleep sitting up because mucus was forming in my mouth that would choke me every hour or so. I was in a zone for weeks, and if it hadn't have been for Sheilah, I don't think I would have survived. I know I would not have."

By the time the biopsy had identified the cancer in Bear's neck, it had already crushed a nerve. Although the preferred method of treatment at the time in America for this form of cancer was surgery, Bear boarded a plane for the three-hour flight to Sydney, where Starfinder stayed with him for a month as Bear began undergoing a grueling series of radiation treatments.

"What they did was push me to within an inch of dying. Over seven weeks, five days a week, they gave me seven grays of radiation. A gray is a hundred rads [i.e., "radiation absorbed dose"]. It's twice what the body can tolerate in a single dose. If they give you thirty-five rads inside of an hour, you're dead in two weeks.

; ; "Over seven weeks, they gave me seven hundred rads and it knocked the living shit out of me. My body was fighting it all the while I was getting it, and as soon as it stopped, my body said, 'Whew, that's over,' but it was really hard for me to get out of bed."

Although the radiation killed the cancer, the aftereffects would alter Bear's life until the day he died. Three years after completing the treatment, he said, "Half my throat still doesn't work. It's hard for me to swallow food because I have no saliva and just one vocal cord, and so when I eat, stuff goes up my nose. I basically have to drink all my food because chewing it creates little particles that cling to my mouth for hours and are hard to wash out.

"I can't open my mouth very well, and all the muscles in my neck are shortened. The radiation also reset my biological clock. I now weigh thirty pounds less than I did before the treatment. I carry almost no body fat and look like an anatomy lesson. My muscles are smaller and it's been hard for me to get back into a proper exercise regime. Permanent damage has been done to my body, and I will never recover fully from the treatment. Almost all my beard is gone. I have no whiskers on the side of my face and neck, and an edema that won't go away. But I'm still here, aren't I?"

Better than anyone else, Sheilah understood how deeply every aspect of Bear's life had been affected by all the radiation. "All the while Bear was going through the treatment, he would say to me, 'My body created this, and with the help of my mind, my body can destroy it.' After finishing his cancer treatment, Bear was so glad to finally have it over. He was also truly spent but determined to make it.

"As time passed, he realized that the quality of his life had been profoundly jeopardized by the treatment. In 2005, they knew how much radiation would kill you, but had not yet figured out how much was just enough. I feel that Bear was overradiated. Perhaps someone made a mistake in the calculations, taking him too close to the threshold. He suffered enormous damage from the radiation as well as the chemo.

"Bear was determined to get his health back and he tried hard and was very brave about it. He had lost a lot of weight and was very tired, and it was obvious that he had a long road back to recovery to even get close to attaining the kind of health he had previously enjoyed. It was devastating to both of us."

Despite his physical limitations, Bear continued to work on improving his property while producing just as much art as he possibly could. Just as obsessive as he had always been, Bear also turned his attention to other pursuits, most notably ridding his land of the toxic *Bufo marinus* toads that had been introduced into Australia in 1935 in a vain attempt to control the greyback cane beetle.

Weighing more than two pounds and phenomenally ugly, the mature female toads could lay over a thousand eggs at a time and were so toxic that if a dog picked one up in its mouth, the dog would be dead in thirty minutes. Because the toads had begun breeding and then poisoning the fish in Bear's acre-and-a-half lake, he would go out at night during the summer months, shine a light on them, and then reach down to pick up each toad with his hands "like you would pick strawberries."

After spraying them "with a Lysol-like material called Det-Sol, which is highly toxic to them," Bear would drop them in a bucket and then dump them all in the woods the next day. In a single night, he might kill as many as 225 toads. During a single month, Bear destroyed 1,400 toads. "Every one I caught couldn't come back and lay more eggs. And if the eggs hatched, I'd throw the tadpoles onto the ground and stomp on them."

In a court filing to appeal the assessed value of his property, Bear would later estimate that from 2004 to 2007, he had killed 3,803 poisonous toads on his land. Rebutting what was then a popular myth about the toads, he also said, "By the way, the venom does not get you high. It does not contain a psychedelic. None. Zero. Zilch."

In 2005, Bear was delighted to learn he had been given what he always considered to be the single greatest honor of his life. "Do you know my name is in the *Oxford English Dictionary?* I guess it was so commonly used on the street in England to describe an exceptionally pure and potent form of LSD that they put it in there as a noun with a lowercase *o.* An *owsley.*

"There are not many people whose names are nouns. There's the guy who jumped off the Brooklyn Bridge and survived, which is called *taking a Brody,* but that's in the vernacular, not in the dictionary. I mean, it's been forty-odd years since I had anything to do with making acid, so it really floored me. I mean, it literally blew my fucking mind."

By then, Bear was well aware that his most enduring legacy would be the massive collection of sonic journals he had recorded during his time on the road with the Grateful Dead. "I think they should release every one of them because the period when I was their soundman was their peak and their golden age, and my recordings are so far superior to everyone else's."

Although he had "no clue" as to how many tapes his collection comprised, they were all being stored in Santa Rosa, California. "I didn't want them in the hands of any record company. I said, 'And what happens if I die? How are my kids going to get them?' Besides, I was not about to sell any of my analog tapes. Those are mine. I mean, Garcia didn't sell his guitar. He sold the music from it.

"I sell the music off those tapes, which I mixed and reflect my production values, and I get them digitized and I give that to the record company, and that is all they get. They don't get the actual analog tapes because those are priceless. They are artifacts. Some are cassettes and some are seven-inch two-track reel-to-reel. Nothing lasts, so eventually they will all have to be converted to digital and then archived, but that takes a lot of time and a good deal of money."

Despite having regularly journeyed from Australia to America for years, Bear had scarcely traveled anywhere else except while on the road with the Grateful Dead. In 2007, his old friend John Meyer, whose sound company had become phenomenally successful, gave Bear and Sheilah a pair of first-class tickets to fly around the world.

And so it was that after they had spent a month journeying from Australia to Bangkok, London, Amsterdam, Zurich, Bern, Florence, Barcelona, Milan, Paris, Boston, New York, Washington, DC, Saratoga Springs, and Los Angeles, I finally met Bear in person for the first time.

21

A Visit from Bear

On a day in May 2007 when the fog on the coast of California was so thick that no one would see the blue moon scheduled to appear that evening, Bear and Sheilah Stanley were getting ready to leave the quaint and charming motel in which they had spent the night after driving up from Los Angeles.

Although the posted checkout time was 11:00 a.m. and it was now well past one o'clock, Bear seemed in no great hurry to vacate his room even though a young woman from the front desk had already knocked twice on the door to remind him that she needed to get someone in there right now to clean up.

All things considered, it might have been far better for everyone that Bear had carried on both of those conversations without ever opening the door. Having turned up the heat in the room so high that it felt like a tropical greenhouse, Bear was stark naked. Stalking back and forth like an emperor who needed no clothes, he just

Bear and Sheilah in Florence, Italy, on May 13, 2007, during their trip around the world. *(©Amalie R. Rothschild)*

kept doggedly sorting through the astonishing array of electronic devices, small appliances, and gear strewn across the floor, all of which he had only recently purchased here in America.

Having lost all the muscle mass that he had worked so hard to develop over the years, Bear had been reduced to literally nothing but skin and bone. For someone who was seventy-two, he did however still look to be in tremendous physical shape. Amazingly cut, the outline of each and every muscle in his body was clearly visible beneath the skin. With a full goatee and a $4,000 hearing aid as well as a small gold earring in his left ear, Bear in person was a worn, elflike man who had the distracted air of a world-class surgeon or some famous professor of literature.

Utterly focused on the task at hand, Bear finally found what he had been looking for. Dumping a handful of the coffee beans he had grown on his property into a large, state-of-the-art conical burr grinder, Bear loudly reduced them to a fine powder. Filling a small white funnel-shaped device with water from the bathroom tap, Bear then began packing up his Braun food mixer and his beard trimmer as he waited patiently for the water to boil.

As soon as it had done so, Bear poured the water into a conical filter mounted on a ceramic cup. Opening up a cooler packed with blue ice, he took out a small container of raw cream from Whole Foods to top off what by any standard known to man had to rank as the world's most perfectly brewed cup of coffee.

Explaining that he needed to drink this right now because he and Sheilah had been denied the free breakfast that came with the room after having arrived three minutes after the dining room had closed this morning, Bear promptly knocked the cup of coffee over onto the carpet. He then spent an inordinate amount of time mopping it all back up again. Having never cared about punctuality, Bear had now made being late an integral part of his lifestyle.

During his extended voyage around the world, Bear had missed nearly every flight on which he and Sheilah had been booked. In a vain attempt to find out where he was and why he hadn't yet arrived, the friends with whom Bear was scheduled to stay had been calling one another constantly.

Three days after he was supposed to have been here, Bear finally began putting on a pair of jeans, which were now two sizes too big on him. Taking one last sip of his coffee, he headed toward the door. Sheilah, who was the soul of patience with Bear and always completely solicitous of his well-being, sighed softly and said, "I've learned to go with the flow. And these days, the flow is very slow."

Stepping outside the motel, Bear pulled a brown Thinsulate stocking cap over his protuberant gremlinlike ears. With his gold earring, dark brown goatee, and the cap, he looked an older, careworn version of the Edge from U2. Pausing for a moment before the rented car in which he had already been stopped by the police for driving erratically, Bear began lamenting that his inability to swallow solid food had now made it impossible for him to enjoy the social joys of eating with others. Suddenly, his eyes reddened and he was nearly reduced to tears. Resolutely reeling himself back in, he said, "But, hey, I'm alive, right?"

As soon as he had swept into my office, Bear immediately made the space entirely his own. Utterly focused on what he was doing, Bear did not notice that he had just used my favorite coffee cup as a receptacle for the protein-rich, soupy mixture that now sustained him. Composed in part of a gelatinous paste that Bear had made by boiling down countless chicken legs, it was not something that anyone would ever have eaten by choice.

Slurping up the stuff as he lowered himself onto the couch, Bear opened an aluminum briefcase that fastened with a lock. The outside of the briefcase was festooned with wrinkled rock 'n' roll stickers. The Grateful Dead at the Dean Smith Center at the University of North Carolina on March 24, 1993. The Who. Jackson Browne. The Grateful Dead at Wembley Stadium in London on October 3, 1990. Good Ole Grateful Dead. The dancing bears. And, of course, the Stealie, which he had helped create.

On the inside lid of the briefcase, Bear had pasted a multitude of his backstage passes one on top of another in layers, thereby creating a road map of where he had been. Methodically, he began sorting through the impossible jumble of items that his briefcase contained. In no particular order, Bear brought out several small and exquisite pieces of his jewelry, the black felt boards on which they could be viewed, a high-powered jeweler's loupe, numerous rolls of tape, a portable memory drive, a small metric scale, a plethora of tiny plastic film canisters, and $10,000 worth of scraps from the gold and platinum coins he had used to make his carvings.

As he scrolled through digital images of his work on his laptop while talking about the pieces that he had sold to Christine McVie of Fleetwood Mac and a host of others, Bear began burning a CD of Big Brother and the Holding Company live at the Carousel Ballroom. No doubt taking notice of my reaction to the way in which Bear had laid waste to my entire office in no time flat, Sheilah kindly offered me some DHEA. When I asked her what it was for, she said, "Stress."

Rooting through his briefcase yet again, Bear produced the

doctor's letter that allowed him as a cancer survivor to board airplanes with all forms of food as well as bottles of water that no one else would have been permitted to bring with them. After handing me a film canister containing some of the high-grade weed he had grown on his property in Australia and then blithely carried with him through customs all over the world, Bear began filling a plastic Baggie with some of the Australian peppercorns that he considered to be the finest in the world.

Not so much a stranger in a strange land as a creature who was completely at home in a world in which no one else had ever dwelled, Bear started talking about the extensive profile of him I had been working on for months that was scheduled to run in the fortieth-anniversary "Summer of Love" issue of *Rolling Stone* magazine in six weeks' time.

Although I had already spent countless hours talking to Bear on the phone from Australia and gone through all the lengthy e-mails he had sent me providing yet more information about his various exploits over the years, none of it had prepared me for what it was like to encounter him in person at such close range. Utterly sweet and genuine, Bear was not so much a force of nature as somebody whom no one could control.

Although I had already done my best to communicate this to those at *Rolling Stone* who were trying to help me shepherd the piece to publication, no one there was accustomed to dealing with someone who was unwilling to do virtually anything to appease the magazine. Despite their repeated entreaties, Bear was still just as camera shy as ever and so had steadfastly refused to sit for a current photograph of himself to accompany the article.

For a variety of reasons, most of them related to his continuing efforts to maintain tenure on his land, Bear told me that the
last thing in the world he needed right now was for the Australian
authorities to be reminded that he was once, as the article would
eventually call him, "The King of LSD." Lest I think he was un-
duly paranoid about this, Bear told me that some kid whom he had
met at a Grateful Dead show in 1987 had only recently come walking up his driveway in Australia as though he had just arrived in
the promised land. As always, Bear wanted to be known, but only
in a manner that suited his needs.

After having left my office in ruins, Bear headed off to San Francisco with Sheilah for what he said would be a two-week stay. Five
weeks later, he was sitting barefoot in black jeans and a T-shirt in a
Starbucks in San Rafael in Marin County talking to Joel Selvin of
the *San Francisco Chronicle*. Telling Selvin that two bands he really
liked these days were Wolfmother and the Arctic Monkeys, Bear
said, "Anytime the music on the radio sounds like rubbish, it's time
to take some LSD."

After having attended a show at the Fillmore by his old friends
Jack Casady and Jorma Kaukonen, Bear and Sheilah left for the
airport the next day to board their flight back home to Australia.
They only got as far as Sausalito before Bear realized that he had
left his briefcase containing their tickets at the house in San Anselmo
where they had been staying. Missing yet another flight, they had
to put off their return for another week.

Having seen Bear in action, this was no great surprise. Believing that "there is no past and no future" because "everything exists
only in present time," it had never occurred to him to drive five

minutes out of his way after leaving my office to visit the Monterey Fairgrounds. Forty years earlier, it was there that his high-powered rocket fuel had helped to usher in the all-out careening psychedelic madness that then became known all over the world as the Summer of Love. For Bear, this had just been another day on the road.

22

On the Way Home

❧❦❧

On November 7, 2009, Bear flew to Victoria to address the annual conference held by Entheogenesis Australis, a group formed to promote "open discussion about psychoactive plants and chemicals." In the two years since he and Sheilah had traveled around the world, Bear had aged so dramatically that he now looked truly old for the first time in his life. His graying hair was thin and sparse. His eyes were sunken in his head. The skin on his face was mottled and tightly drawn.

Far thinner than he had ever before been, Bear sat slumped in a chair with a bunch of tissues in one hand as he talked softly into the microphone he was also holding. Although his mind was still as sharp as it had ever been, he looked in every way like a shrunken replica of the physical specimen he had once been.

"Bear did look terrible," Sheilah would later say. "I hadn't realized it at the time, but when I saw the footage later, I was shocked.

He spoke well at the conference and was very well received. The audience loved him, but he looked bad. He still had such an amazing presence and had not lost his joie de vivre. Both Starfinder and I were very proud of him."

Sixteen months later, on Friday, March 11, 2011, Bear and Sheilah flew to Sydney so he could visit his oncologist for his final checkup to ensure that he had been cancer-free for five years. As always when they traveled these days, Bear and Sheilah missed a couple of flights, and so she was particularly exhausted by the time that they finally checked into their hotel room.

As Sheilah began filling the tub so she could take a bath, Bear carefully extracted a cotton string from the room's Oriental carpet. Putting the string into a dish, he poured a ring of oil around it, pulled up the stem of the string, and lit it. He then brought the glowing dish into the bathroom so Sheilah would have a candle by the bathtub.

"I was deeply touched by the gesture. We'd both had a really rough time of it that day, and he encouraged me to relax in a bath and let the day go and then surprised me with this candle he had made for me. It really was one of the sweetest, most romantic things he had ever done for me, and I appreciated how clever and inventive he was. There were so many beautiful things he did for me that, looking back on it now, I can see how much love he had for me and how he showed it in so many ways. We really loved one another."

The next day, Bear received what for him was both good and bad news. The good news was that he was still cancer-free. The bad news was that when Bear asked the doctor if stem-cell treatment could help him, his reply was "No." "You know," Bear told the doctor, "anyone else who had just gotten the news you've given me would be in a fetal position in the corner. But I'm not going to let it get me down. I'm going to go with this and do whatever I can to get my life back."

Just before Bear and Sheilah boarded their return flight to Cairns, he suddenly said, "Hold on a minute. I'll be right back." Running into a store in the airport, Bear returned holding a card with a big heart on it and said, "I want to give this to you. I love you." As Sheilah later recalled, "There was just something about that day. As though he had a sixth sense about what was going to happen."

By the time they arrived in Cairns, Bear's daughter Redbird and her husband had already brought Sheilah's Toyota Land Cruiser station wagon from their home to the airport. Although Bear had the keys to the car with him, he lost them at the airport, and he and Sheilah had to spend some time searching before he found them again. After they finally got into the car, Bear decided he wanted to go buy something. Sheilah told him it was already getting late, but Bear drove to a stereo store only to learn that it had already closed for the day.

Although their original plan had been to visit Redbird and perhaps spend the night with her in Cairns, she had only recently given birth to twin boys. Since it was now dinnertime and "pandemonium at their house," Sheilah said, "Let's just go home." After calling Redbird to let her know what they were doing, Bear began heading north on the Kennedy Highway.

Nearly two hours later, as they drove through the rain up the steep, winding road past Davies Creek on their way home, Bear heard Miles Davis playing on the radio. As he reached over to turn up the volume, the Land Cruiser hit an oil slick. Bear lost control of the wheel, and the station wagon slid into a deep pool of mud and water on the side of the road. Flipping sideways, the vehicle then slammed into a large ironbark tree on Sheilah's side of the car. Although Bear had always liked to drive as fast as possible, he had not been doing so before the accident.

Because the roof of the car had collapsed and the dashboard had flown up between them, Sheilah couldn't not see Bear, but she could still hear him. It was starting to get dark and the rain was really pouring down. Sheilah kept calling out for Bear, but he did not answer. A team of paramedics quickly arrived on the scene. As one of them began putting a brace on Sheilah's neck, she said, "No, no, no. I want you to pay attention to my husband. He's not responding. I'm okay. Please just pay attention to him. He needs your help."

After the paramedics began working on Bear, one of them told Sheilah that they had gotten a heartbeat, and she said, "Well, that's really good." As the car had begun sliding across the road, Bear had put his arm across the seat to protect Sheilah from the impact. She had then continued to hold on to his hand while calling out his name without getting any response. Sheilah herself was trapped in the front seat of the totaled car for an hour as the rescue team worked to cut her from the wreckage.

"Suddenly after a few more minutes, I noticed that no one was saying anything. It was very quiet and I felt that something was wrong. 'What's going on?' I said. 'What's happening? Why aren't you looking after my husband? I don't need you. He does.' Sounding annoyed by my questions, the paramedic finally said, 'He's dead.'

"This was from a paramedic! Someone who was supposed to feel compassion and know just what to say at such a time. He just told me that flat out, and I could not understand how someone could be so heartless. I was stunned. I became very quiet and could not believe what I had just heard. How could Bear be dead? He couldn't be dead. It was just horrible. Absolutely horrible.

"I had just been given the news that my husband was dead. I did not want to leave. I wanted to stay right there until they came to get him. I felt like my heart had been torn out and I refused to move. I had just lost everything that meant anything to me. I could not even cry. I just sat there in disbelief. Finally, a very lovely fireman came and spoke to me so gently and kindly. Like a rag doll, I reluctantly followed his instructions.

"For the longest time afterwards I just kept thinking that Bear would come driving down the driveway. That it had all just been a bad dream and he was going to come driving down that driveway just like he had always done before."

That Sheilah had escaped relatively unscathed from the accident seemed like a miracle to those who saw the wreck. Luckily, she had been wedged in the only place in the car where anyone could have survived. Perhaps the only mercy about any of it was that Bear had only recently said that he would not know what to do if Sheilah passed away before him.

Having flown to Australia a few days before the accident with his wife so that he could introduce Bear to his one-year-old granddaughter, Starfinder had spent some time with his father before Bear and Sheilah had flown to Sydney. After learning about the accident, Starfinder called his mother, who was in India, and she flew to Australia as well.

Bear's funeral was held on March 22, 2011, at a time when his friends in California could watch it on Skype. Sam Cutler, who as the road manager for the Rolling Stones had been involved in hiring the Hells Angels to act as security at Altamont, flew from Sydney to attend the service. Bear's daughter Nina was also there, as were Melissa Cargill and her husband.

Draped with flowers from his property, Bear's coffin was also adorned with the Grateful Dead skull logo and thirteen-point lightning bolt that Starfinder had drawn. An illustrated program with Bear's artwork was handed out at the service as "Black Peter" from *Bear's Choice* and "Attics of My Life" from *American Beauty* played in the background.

Sheilah had called Robert Hunter's wife, Maureen, in California to ask if they had heard the news. After Maureen Hunter told her that they had, Sheilah asked, "'Do you think Robert would consider writing an eulogy for Bear?' And she said, 'Of course he would. I think that's a great idea.' And he did. He sent something to me within a day. He must have gotten right on it or maybe it had been filtering through his mind ever since he had heard the news and he was prepared, and he e-mailed it to me."

At Bear's funeral, Starfinder read the fifty-three-line free-verse epitaph, entitled "An Anthem for the Bear." The concluding lines read:

> *Was there ever a man who changed so many*
> *while, himself, changing so little?*
> *A Cardinal sign, were there ever one*
> *fixed like a bright white star in dark-blue heaven.*
> *Save sentimental eulogies for lesser men*
> *and leave it that he was the King of Many Things*
> *of perfected personal taste and detailed opinion*
> *first and last a scientist and a propounder*
> *of a brand new species of reason*

No bucolic Heaven for such as Bear,
rather a Rock of Ages from where
an eagle in full flight might dare
a sudden detour into endless dawn.
Sail on, dear brother Bear, sail on.

When he died on a rain-slicked highway in Australia, the land where he had gone to escape the ice-age storm that he was convinced would lay waste to the entire northern hemisphere, Augustus Owsley Stanley III, aka Bear, was seventy-six years old.

Epilogue

More Anthems for the Bear

❦

Not surprisingly, many of those who had known and loved Bear first learned of his death on the Internet, the medium he himself had so quickly embraced as his preferred method of communication with the world at large. John Perry Barlow seems to have been the first to spread the news in a tweet in which he described Bear as an "Acid King, Annealer of the Grateful Dead, and Master Crank" who "died with his boots on."

Four years earlier, Barlow had said of his old comrade-in-arms, "He is as American as apple pie. Bear has always been exactly the same age. The main thing to know about Augustus Owsley Stanley III is that his trajectory through life has been flatter than any other person I have ever known. In his essence, he has been undeviatingly himself. Even though battered by the most astonishing winds of change and fashion and frippery and ups and downs and deaths and rebirths and marriages and madness, he has always maintained himself in precisely this configuration. And although I always know exactly what he is going to say about goddamn everything, that doesn't spare him from saying it anyway."

The day after Bear died, Phil Lesh, who had always been Bear's closest ally in the Grateful Dead, posted a eulogy on the Internet entitled "A Beautiful Mind." In part, it said, "Bear, for me, was a true kindred spirit; when we first met, it was as if I had met a long-lost brother from another lifetime. I am heartbroken and devastated at his passing.

"He was a friend, a brother, an inspiration, and our patron at the very beginning of our creative lives. We owe him more than can be counted or added up—his was a mind that refused to accept limits, and he reinforced in us that striving for the infinite, the refusal to accept the status quo, that has informed so much of our work. . . .

"A mind like Bear's appears only very rarely, and it's been my privilege and honor to have known and loved two such minds— Jerry and Bear. . . . I am eternally grateful for all of the gifts Bear brought to the scene and to the music. Fare thee well; I love you more than words can tell."

The extensive coverage that Bear's passing generated through-out the world in what had once been known as "the straight media" would have delighted no one more than Bear himself. *The Australian* in his adopted homeland, as well as *The Telegraph*, *The Guardian*, and *The Independent* newspapers in the United Kingdom, all ran lengthy obituaries of him.

The New York Times devoted twenty-two paragraphs to a full-blown account of Bear's life and times, accompanied by the iconic Rosie McGee photo of Bear in a slouch hat standing beside a bushy-haired and thickly bearded Jerry Garcia with a cigarette dangling from his mouth. Two days later, the newspaper ran a long personal reminiscence of Bear on the first page of its Arts section entitled, "Heads Bowed in Grateful Memory." Bear was memorialized yet again in the annual issue of *The New York Times Sunday Magazine* that celebrates the lives of those of note who have passed away during the previous year.

In an article entitled "The Dead Recall the Colorful Life of LSD Pioneer Owsley Stanley" in *Rolling Stone* magazine, Mickey Hart told David Browne, "I never thought the Bear would die. He was too tough and ornery. But his neck was almost bone because of the chemo. . . . The last time I saw him, he was pureeing meat in a veggie mixer so he could drink it through a straw. At least now Jerry and Pigpen will have someone to talk to. They're yucking it up together, wherever 'there' is."

As always, the last word about Bear's life rightfully belongs to Bear. As he said in 2007, "I tend to be overwhelming, so people put me out of their heads. It's too challenging and too frightening to get me. Sometimes being me is like living in the quiet center of a tornado or a hurricane. And I'm the only thing not spinning around. But the universe does get at me, though.

"I wish it were true that I was innocent with no evil intent and not ego driven because that's mastery, which has always been my goal. I admire the master because if you master something, you don't even think about it anymore. It becomes as simple and natural as breathing or riding a bicycle. That's the way it is with me. Whether it's sculpture or sound mixing or anything else, I don't think about it. I just turn a few knobs and everything automatically does what it's supposed to do."

After his funeral, Bear was cremated, and some of his ashes were scattered on his property. When the Grateful Dead performed their fiftieth anniversary "Fare Thee Well" shows at Soldier Field in Chicago on July 3, 4, and 5, 2015, Starfinder brought a jar containing a portion of his father's ashes with him and placed it on the sound board so Bear could once again be with the band he had always loved as much as life itself.

While Bear's true final resting place would always be in the music that he had done all he could to help the Grateful Dead create, the trajectory of his utterly unconventional yet completely American life spoke volumes about the limits of personal freedom in this country. An outlier from birth who became an outlaw in the eyes of a society that perceived him as a distinct threat to the status quo, Bear was someone to whom the ordinary rules of behavior never applied.

Despite his many glaring flaws, Bear was always so absolutely fearless in so many ways that Jerry Garcia called him a hero. At a crucial turning point in the history of this country, this was precisely the role he came to play for many who also considered themselves outcasts in the nation where they had been born.

While the powerful substance he manufactured in bulk and with which his name will always be linked has caused a multitude of problems, it also brought about significant social change by opening people's minds to a reality they would otherwise never have encountered. That same substance has continued to influence the culture even in our current digital age.

Steve Jobs, who did as much as anyone to create the high-tech world in which we now all live, famously said that taking LSD was "a profound experience." Calling it "one of the two or three most important things" he had ever done in his life, Jobs added that people who had not tried psychedelics could never understand some things about him.

Although Bear never would have been totally on board with that statement, neither man would have agreed with the other about anything else. But then, Bear himself would never have had it any other way.

Appendix

Bear's Choice:
A Selected Discography

s Bear himself so proudly noted in 2005 on his Web site, he had by then been credited with having recorded thirteen albums, as well as five collections on which his sonic journals comprised anywhere from three cuts to 63 percent of the total content.

After Bear's death in 2011, his family established the Owsley Stanley Foundation to preserve the vast archive of tapes that he had left behind. By eventually releasing them for sale, the foundation hopes to generate what Sheilah Stanley called "enough money to support kids who want to study any form of art, music, recording, and dance as well as fund community outreach programs for music and sound."

Over his long career both on and off the road with the Grateful Dead, Bear recorded more than thirteen hundred live performances on cassettes as well as reel-to-reel tapes. Although no complete list of

the archive's contents has yet been made available, bands such as
the Jefferson Airplane, Quicksilver Messenger Service, Country Joe
and the Fish, Love, Blue Cheer, and Fleetwood Mac all opened for
the Dead, and so Bear recorded their performances as well.

The foundation's Web site also notes that the collection includes
"rare recordings" of live performances by Miles Davis, Johnny
Cash, Santana, Taj Mahal, Ramblin' Jack Elliott, Thelonious
Monk, the Electric Flag, the Youngbloods, Chuck Berry, and Big
Brother and the Holding Company among others.

Although Bear initially began taping Grateful Dead shows so
that he and the band could then listen to them to improve what they
were all doing onstage, he always took great pains to record the
band just as they sounded during each performance. Because Bear
never altered or manipulated what had been played onstage during
a show, his tapes represent a sonically accurate picture of what it
was like to have heard all this music as it was being made.

Because all of the tapes are now nearing the end of their shelf
life and will probably degrade within the next five years, the Owsley
Stanley Foundation has launched an online fund-raising drive to
preserve them "for the public benefit, to be appreciated by genera-
tions of musicians, fans, historians, ethnomusicologists, sound engineers, and others."

The foundation hopes to raise $300,000 to $400,000 to pay for
the two to four years of studio time that sound engineers will need
to digitize all of Bear's sonic journals. Donations can be made to the
Owsley Stanley Foundation via PayPal.

Following is a list of all the recordings Bear made that were released while he was still alive, as well as one that came out after his
death. They are listed here in the same order in which they appear

on Bear's Web site along with some of his comments as well as what others had to say about them.

1. *Bear's Choice* (**Warner Bros., 1973**)—The first album made from his live recordings, *Bear's Choice* consists of excerpts from two shows by the Grateful Dead at the Fillmore East in New York City on February 13 and 14, 1970, as well as three tracks they had recorded about a week earlier at the Fillmore West in San Francisco. With the Allman Brothers as the opening act and Love playing second on the bill at the Fillmore East shows, Bear remembered those performances as "extra nice as the mixing board and the hall were sweet-sounding."

2. *Allman Brothers Band Live at the Fillmore East, 1970* (**Grateful Dead Records, 1997**)—Recorded by Bear thirteen months before the Allman Brothers cut *Live at the Fillmore*, which is still considered one of the greatest live albums ever made in the history of rock, this release is a compilation of tracks by the Allman Brothers from shows featuring the Dead as headliners on February 11, 13, and 14, 1970.

In his liner notes for the album, Bear wrote that since his taping efforts were "always secondary to the task of running the house system," he could not give his full attention to his tape mix. "The demands of the hall frequently led to the tape running out in the middle of songs and stuff like that, but there was little I could do, since I didn't have an assistant."

3. *Dick's Picks, Volume 4* (**Grateful Dead Records, 1996**)—This album consists of more tracks culled from the same shows that had formed the basis of *Bear's Choice*. With both the Allman Brothers and the Grateful Dead jamming endlessly as Love did a forty-five-minute set between the two bands, Bear noted that the Saturday-night show at Fillmore East did not end until 5:58 A.M. on Sunday.

While Bear always had great respect for the Allman Brothers, he was far less impressed by Love. Because he "had no real interest in keeping them in my diary—so with the vain hope they would improve, I used the same reel of tape over—thus I only have the last show."

Although there was always an early show at the Fillmore East and then a late show that began at 11:30 P.M., Bear took great pains to explain that by this time the Grateful Dead had told Bill Graham that they would only do one show a night there.

In his liner notes for the album, Bear wrote, "The performance was always more important than getting the tape right. The first few songs usually weren't as well mixed on the tape as those which came after I had the house up and running smoothly."

4. *Steal Your Face* **(Grateful Dead Records, 1976)**— Recorded by five different sound engineers on October 16, 17, 18, 19, and 20, 1974, at Bill Graham's Winterland Ballroom in San Francisco during what was then called the Dead's "farewell run" of shows before they went on hiatus for the next two years, Bear considered this album "one I would just as soon forget.

"The master tapes were a disaster of major proportions, requiring a complete over dubbing of all the vocals and many of the instrumental tracks. I had absolutely nothing to do with the recording of the master tapes, and was called in to try to 'fix it.' Phil Lesh and I were given only 18 days to rebuild this *'Titanic.'* Fact is, of course, no-one could make a silk purse out of this pig's ear."

Or, as Jerry Garcia noted, "None of us liked it. I'm sure even Phil and Owsley didn't like it that much. I think part of it was that we were not working, and we didn't have anything else to deliver."

5. *Old and in the Way* (Round Records/Sugar Hill/ RykoDisc/Grateful Dead Records, 1975)—Recorded live by Bear and Vickie Babcock at the Boarding House in San Francisco on October 8, 1973, and then mixed and produced by David Grisman, this album consists of ten songs, one of which is a cover version of the Rolling Stones' "Wild Horses."

Bear wrote that the show presented him with the "wonderful opportunity to try the various ideas I had about the production of a realistic stereo sound from multiple microphones." By clipping eight omnidirectional microphones, none of which fed into the PA, onto the stands in front of the musicians, Bear was able to "capture a stereo 'space,' which while different from the actual onstage sound, gives the listener the impression of being in amongst the performers. . . . Something like a hologram is how I like to think of it."

6. *That High Lonesome Sound* (Acoustic Disc, 1996)—Recorded by Bear and Vickie Babcock on October 1, 1973, at the Boarding House in San Francisco and produced by David Grisman, this album consists of fourteen Old and in the Way tracks, including a version of "Orange Blossom Special." As Bear noted, "It was a learning experience for me, coupled with the usual sound-in-the-hall difficulties facing a band playing small venues. It is too bad that the band didn't continue for a while longer."

7. *Breakdown* (Acoustic Disc, 1998)—Yet a third album of Old and in the Way performing live at the Boarding House. "I didn't think there were that many songs but here it is. . . . So much for my memory of events over 25 years ago. . . . No, I am NOT going to blame it on 'the drugs.' (I seem to remember we did do some from time to time in those days.)"

8. *Fallout from the Phil Zone* (Grateful Dead Records, 1995)—A double album consisting of eleven live performances by the Grateful Dead that had been selected by Phil Lesh. Bear calculated that 63 percent of them came from his sonic journals, which would somehow mean that he had recorded 6.93 of the tracks. The version of "New Speedway Boogie" comes from a rehearsal that Bear had taped.

Although he was then no longer a member of the Grateful Dead crew, Bear recorded the band's prolonged version of "In the Midnight Hour" on September 3 or 4, 1969, at the Dance Hall in Rio Nido, a small unincorporated community on the Russian River in Sonoma County, California.

Bear taped the performance in two separate channels, one for vocals and the other for instruments, and "the two signals have a natural time difference. The ear interprets this as space. Phil resolved this difficulty by mixing to mono. I probably would have tried a digital technique in an attempt to preserve the spatiality, but unfortunately I was not consulted during the album's preparation."

9. *Dick's Picks, Volume 11* (Grateful Dead Records, 1998)—Recorded at the Stanley Theater in Jersey City, New Jersey, on September 27, 1972, by Bear and Bob Matthews, the three-disc set consists of twenty-five songs. "I Know You, Rider" contains a patched cut from another show. Bear had little to say about this release.

10. *So Many Roads* (Grateful Dead Records, 1999)—A five-disc box set containing thirty-two live performances recorded over twenty-five years, the collection was also released to the media as a one-disc sampler. Bear recorded all of the songs on the first disc as well as one track on the second. The royalties Bear earned from his work on *So Many Roads,* which was certified as a gold record in April 2000, would have been yet another source of significant income for him in Australia.

11. *Dick's Picks, Volume 16* **(Grateful Dead Records, 1999)**—Recorded by Bear on November 8, 1969, in the Fillmore Auditorium (which was then no longer being operated by Bill Graham), the album consists of twenty-three songs and features the first live performance of "Cumberland Blues."

Although Bear did not remember much about the show, he did recall going to the Rolling Stones' performance at the Oakland Coliseum the following night. After the Stones had blown out their Ampeg amps during the first show, three members of the Dead's road crew drove to San Francisco and returned "just in the nick of time for the Stones to go on after Ike and Tina's opener. Personally, I thought they sounded a lot better on the Fenders than their somewhat wimpy amps."

Noting that he then did the sound for the Stones' disastrous free concert at Altamont, Bear added, "And yes, I do have a sonic journal of that gig too."

12. *Dick's Picks, Volume 23* **(Grateful Dead Records, 2001)**—Recorded by Bear on September 17, 1972, at the Baltimore Civic Center in Baltimore, Maryland, this three-disc set consisting of twenty-three songs, among them a nearly forty-minute version of "The Other One," was most definitely not one of his favorites.

"This concert was not chosen by me. In fact I was not told it was in preparation until after it was finished. I had no input and I don't have any liner notes on it." None too pleased that due to lack of space, the band's encore "One More Saturday Night" was not included on the second disc, Bear also noted, "I have been told that whenever one of my tapes is to be made into an album in the future, it will be with my full participation, so this sort of thing should end here."

13. *The Golden Road* (Grateful Dead Records, 2001)—A massive twelve-CD box set consisting of 163 tracks that include remastered versions of all the albums that the Dead had recorded while under contract to Warner Bros. Records, *The Golden Road* cost more than $100 when it was released.

Although the twelfth CD was a reissue of *Bear's Choice*, Bear wrote on his Web site that "about 40% of the bonus tracks are taken from my sonic journals. I was awarded my second gold record for participating in this compilation."

14. *Dick's Picks, Volume 25* (Grateful Dead Records, 2001)—This four-CD set consisting of thirty-five songs was recorded by Bear and Betty Cantor-Jackson on May 10, 1978, at the Veterans Memorial Coliseum in New Haven, Connecticut, and at the Springfield Civic Center Arena in Springfield, Massachusetts, on May 11, 1978. Among the tracks is a rare version of the Dead covering Warren Zevon's "Werewolves of London."

Bear taped the show in New Haven on a day off while he was on the road with Robert Hunter and Comfort. After having arrived at the show with his Nagra and a couple of reels of blank tape, Bear "was able to convince Betty Cantor, who was at that time the Dead's recordist, to allow me the use of a pair of unused busses on her recording board. . . . In this package you will have the unique opportunity to directly compare my technique with that of Betty on consecutive shows, using identical resources to mix from. It is a perfect representation of our distinctly different mixing philosophies."

15. *Dick's Picks, Volume 26* (Grateful Dead Records, 2001)—Recorded by Bear on April 26, 1969, at the Electric Theater in Chicago, Illinois, and on April 27, 1969, at the Labor Temple in Minneapolis, Minnesota, the twenty-seven songs on this release include a rare Grateful Dead cover of Jimmy Reed's "I Know It's a Sin."

As Bear pointed out in his liner notes, "1969 was a year of contrasts, including Woodstock and Altamont for example. We were still pretty new at the R&R touring game and we played in all sorts of halls. On tour, we rarely could afford separate hotel rooms for everyone, so we shared, something which seems very odd, looking back, but I think it was one of the nicer things limited money did, because we got to know each other pretty well that way."

16. *Grateful Dead Rare Cuts and Oddities, 1966* (Grateful Dead Records, 2005)—Recorded by Bear at a variety of shows during that year, the eighteen tracks include the Dead doing Rufus Thomas's "Walking the Dog," Chuck Berry's "Promised Land," Johnny "Guitar" Watson's "Gangster of Love," Slim Harpo's "I'm a King Bee," the Rolling Stones' "Empty Heart," as well as "Good Lovin'," a number-one hit for the Young Rascals in 1966.

"For me it was very much a unique and strange year. I met the Grateful Dead that year and became their sound man. Of all the interesting and wonderful things that I have had an opportunity to do in my life so far, it ranks at the very top of the list. The Dead were young and raw, full of a special kind of energy. They had been a band for only about six months and most of their repertoire was covers—but what an eclectic and odd bunch of covers they were.

I don't think there has ever been anything quite like them, before or since."

17. *Dick's Picks, Volume 36* **(Grateful Dead Records, 2005)**—The final installment in the series, this four-CD set contains the complete show by the Dead that Bear recorded at the Spectrum in Philadelphia, Pennsylvania, on September 21, 1972, as well as three bonus tracks from the band's show at Folsom Field in Boulder, Colorado, on September 3, 1972. The thirty songs include a cover version of Marty Robbins's "El Paso" as well as a thirty-seven-minute-long "Dark Star."

"1972 saw my return to the band after an absence of two years. The year was exciting for me although I was having some problems with the crew, many of whom had come to work after I had gone, and resented my efforts to improve things on stage and with the equipment. . . . The various problems, particularly the one of getting those who did my job while I was away to back off and allow me to return to my work, eventually inspired me to design the Wall of Sound. . . . The hassles themselves did not interfere with my ability to mix, and the band played many fine shows during this period—this is a good example."

Fittingly, the caveat emptor for this release reads, "Dick's Picks Vol. 36 was mastered from the original 1/4" analog sonic journal tapes recorded at 7.5 ips, and were not produced with commercial intentions. However, due to the masterful skill of the recordist, these tapes sound remarkably rich and true to the live sound. Being more than thirty years old, the tapes exhibit some minor signs of the ravages of time, as we all do, but rest assured that everything possible has been done to make them sound as good as possible."

18. *Janis Joplin in Concert* **(CBS, 1971)**—Calling this "a complete shambles made of my tapes of a very good performance," Bear noted that three of the songs on this album, "Roadblock," "Flower in the Sun," and "Summertime," were "taken from my tapes which were stored at the Alembic Studios in SF while I was in jail." Elliot Mazer, whose last name Bear misspells as Maser, then remixed them "to 'make them match' the poor quality of the other recordings he was using in the album."

After having learned what had been done to the three songs he had recorded, Bear refused to sign the contract and informed the label that "they must not release the album mixed the way it was." Believing they had already acquired the rights from Dan Healy, CBS went right ahead and did so anyway. Bear then filed a lawsuit against the company, which he eventually agreed to drop in return for "a small royalty."

19. *Big Brother Live at the Carousel Ballroom 1968* **(Columbia/Legacy, 2012)**—Released on the first anniversary of Bear's death, what he believed would "be hailed as the definitive Big Brother live album of all time" was dedicated to his memory. "The sound is much better than I thought it would be, no tape hiss, and no noticeable distortion or evidence of deterioration of the re-cording media. This is surprising considering these tapes are 31 years old and have not always been stored under ideal conditions."

Having worked on bringing this project to fruition right until the time of his death, Bear is credited as the producer, mastering super-visor, sound engineer, and author of the liner notes, to which his son Starfinder, Rhoney Gissen Stanley, and Sheilah Stanley also con-tributed. In Sheilah Stanley's words, "This is Bear's vision—how he heard the band live, and how he wanted to transmit it to you."

The final paragraph in this section of Bear's Web site reads, "I have a lot of tapes stored in the Dead's tape vault. Virtually every band that played on the same bill with the Grateful Dead during my years as soundman and who did not bring their own soundman was recorded. I would be very interested in working with any of the bands concerned to see if the tapes represent anything worth releasing. I will post the list once it is OCR'ed (a big job!)."

Although Bear never got around to doing this before he died, all of the amazing music that he recorded during his lifetime is still right there on those tapes, just waiting to be released.

Acknowledgments

For having gone out and sold this book, I would like to thank my old friend and colleague Paul Bresnick. My thanks go as well to Rob Kirkpatrick, who acquired it for Thomas Dunne Books at St. Martin's Press. Expertly, Peter Wolverton then steered the book to publication. I am truly grateful for his excellent notes as well as all the help he gave me.

Joel Selvin, whose continuing affection for Bear rivals my own, was enthusiastic about this project right from the start, and he made it possible for me to contact Sheilah Stanley. Despite how difficult it still was for her to discuss this with me, I could never have reconstructed the last twenty-four hours of Bear's life without her. For having done so, I offer her my heartfelt thanks.

Charles Perry, with whom I had the pleasure of working at *Rolling Stone* magazine back in the day, was an unending source of invaluable information. Without his willingness to answer all of the many questions that I posed to him, I could never have written this book. I also want to thank him for graciously allowing me to quote so extensively from "Owsley and Me," his incisive article that remains the best firsthand account of what it was to hang out with Bear all those many years ago. I am also deeply indebted to Bear's nephew Michael Manning, whose stunning research provided me with information I could never have found anywhere else.

Not surprisingly considering all the drugs that were then being consumed by those who were part of the scene around the Grateful Dead, the exact chronology of certain events often varies wildly from one source to another. In writing this book, I have relied on Dennis McNally's *A Long Strange Trip: The Inside History of the Grateful Dead* as the absolutely most authoritative guide to when, where, and how these events occurred. For all those who want to know what that long, strange trip was truly like, his book remains essential reading.

I also owe a debt of gratitude to David Browne and I highly recommend his excellent book *So Many Roads: The Life and Times of the Grateful Dead*.

For doing his best to help me locate a photograph of Bear that in the end could not be found, I would like to thank my old friend Ken Turan. I should also like to express my gratitude to Rosie McGee, Amalie R. Rothschild, Ed Perlstein, and Richard Pechner for supplying the photographs that accompany the text. A special thank you to Jay Blakesberg, who came up with the photograph of Owsley, Ravi Shankar, and Ali Akbar Khan taken by Jim Marshall at Monterey Pop.

Closer to home, I would like to extend my continuing gratitude to Donna for putting up with me as I worked my way through Bear's life. As always, big love to Sandy and Anna. While writing about Bear was not easy, I hope even he would recognize that I have done my best to get as much of this as right as I possibly could.

Notes

Epigraph

xi   *I'm not interested*, Bear e-mail, 1/31/2007.

xi   *There's nothing*, Lesh, *Searching for the Sound*.

Prologue: The Muir Beach Acid Test

2   *like the claws of a tiger*, Gans, *Conversations with the Dead*.

2   *bigger than the Beatles*, Bear e-mail, 4/1/2007.

2   *"alchemist, seer, magician,"* Wolfe, *Electric Kool-Aid Acid Test*.

3   *geometrically increases his paranoia*, McNally, *A Long Strange Trip*.

3   *into a ditch*, Bear interview, 1/31/2007.

3   *angels and devils*, ibid.

4   *"No, no,"* Cargill e-mail, 2/18/2007.

4   *"the Johnny Appleseed,"* Lesh, *Searching for the Sound*.

4   *"The Pranksters,"* Bear interview, 1/31/2007.

1. Bluegrass Roots

5   *"an excellent excuse,"* WPA *Guide to Kentucky*.

5   *"the last of,"* Bob Weir interview, 2/27/2007.

5   *Nuddicut Owsley Stanley*, www.historykygovenors.com/aostanley. htm.

7 *"Gentlemen, I beg you,"* ibid.

7 *"We are at war,"* "Augustus Owsley Stanley," McKenzie Martin, http://explorekyhistory.ky.gov.

8 *"I shall give,"* www.historykygovenors.com/aostanley.htm.

8 *"You cannot milk,"* Dorson, *America in Legend.*

8 *frequently mentioned,* Klotter and Schillinger, *Kentucky Profiles.*

9 *"He did not graduate,"* Bear interview, 1/31/2007.

9 *"Then the Depression,"* ibid.

10 *"He transferred into,"* ibid.

11 *"What happened was,"* ibid.

12 *"from this point on,"* "U.S.S. *Lexington*—Action Report of the Battle of the Coral Sea," www.ibiblio.org/hyperwar/USN/ships/logs/CV/CV2-Coral.html.

12 *"The picture of the,"* ibid.

12 *"My father must,"* Bear interview, 1/31/2007.

13 *"My name is not,"* Bear e-mail, 3/27/2007.

2. Growing Up Absurd

15 *"quite get the knack,"* Bear interview, 1/31/2007.

15 *"black nannies whom we,"* ibid.

16 *"I didn't recognize letters,"* Eisner, "Interview with an Alchemist."

16 *"I didn't like,"* Bear interview, 1/31/2007.

16 *"like dog shit,"* ibid.

17 *"to provide for the,"* en.wikipedia.org/wiki/.Charlotte_Hall_Military_Academy.

17 *"The result was,"* Eisner, "Interview with an Alchemist."

17 *"almost like a brainchild,"* *High Times,* February 1979, as quoted by Stevens, *Storming Heaven.*

18 *"I was tossed out,"* Bear interview, 1/31/2007.

19 *"All America is an,"* Mitgang, "Researchers Dispute Ezra Pound's 'Insanity.'"

19 *"I don't know if,"* Bear interview, 1/31/2007.

19 *"it totally freaked out,"* ibid.

20 *"It was hard for me,"* ibid.

20 *"And then, the,"* ibid.

21 *"an incompetent very senior,"* Bear e-mail, 3/27/2007.

21 *"I picked engineering,"* Bear interview, 1/31/2007.

21 *"I was the kind of guy,"* ibid.

22 *"I was terrified of,"* ibid.

22 *"emotionally unbalanced,"* Reasons, "'Mr. LSD' Makes Millions."

22 *"We haven't had,"* ibid.

23 *"He had insulted,"* Bear e-mail, 4/13/2007.

23 *"an old name,"* *Lexington* (Ky.) *Herald,* March 28, 1968.

3. Shape-Shifting

25 *"clown dive,"* Bear interview, 1/31/2007.

25 *"It was my right,"* ibid.

26 *"I wound up,"* Jackson, *Garcia: An American Life.*

26 *"I was twenty-three,"* Bear interview, 1/31/2007.

27 *"I was very,"* ibid.

28 *"just a little,"* Reasons, "'Mr. LSD' Makes Millions."

28 *"I bounced some,"* Eisner, "Interview with an Alchemist."

4. Berkeley, 1964

31 *"Forty-five minutes later,"* Perry, "Owsley and Me."

32 *"boxes full of,"* ibid.

32 *"the most amazing,"* ibid.

32 *"a funky little,"* Eisner, "Interview with an Alchemist."

32 *"a huge stash,"* Perry, "Owsley and Me."

33 *"a quaint cottage,"* Charles Perry e-mail, 6/4/2015.

34 *"her away from,"* ibid.

34 *"a cute little,"* ibid.

34 *"I remember the,"* Bear interview, 1/31/2007.

34 *"And I found,"* Eisner, "Interview with an Alchemist."

35 *"In the early,"* Cargill e-mail, 2/28/2007.

35 *"in a dream-like state,"* Hofmann, *LSD—My Problem Child.*

36 *"enjoy the unprecedented,"* ibid.

36 *"an unusually fragile,"* Shulgin and Shulgin, *TiHKAL.*

37 *"They took one,"* Bear e-mail, 4/13/2007.

37 *"showed up at one,"* Perry, "Owsley and Me."

37 *"In the charges,"* Bear e-mail, 4/13/2007.

37 *"At the time,"* Perry e-mail, 10/16/2015.

38 *"He wanted,"* Perry, "Owsley and Me."

39 *"who reflected,"* ibid.

39 *"at the property,"* ibid.

39 *"'Where is your,'"* ibid.

40 *"overlooked the residue,"* ibid.

40 *"To be honest,"* Cargill e-mail, 3/17/2007.

5. Making Acid

41 *"a nasty brown,"* Bear e-mail, 4/1/2007.

42 *"There's no more,"* Eisner, "Interview with an Alchemist."

43 *"a college kid thing,"* Perry e-mail, 10/15/2015.

43 *"If you were not,"* Bear interview, 1/31/2007.

43 *"I'd take a,"* ibid.

43 *"LSD is something,"* ibid.

44 *"I never, ever,"* Bear e-mail, 4/1/2007.

44 *"difficult to get,"* Bear interview, 1/31/2007.

44 *"dropping some off,"* ibid.

44 *"When you start,"* ibid.

45 *"I started doing,"* ibid.

45 *"I never fronted,"* Bear e-mail, 4/1/2007.

45 *"told people,"* Bear interview, 1/31/2007.

46 *"love to Melissa,"* Stevens, *Storming Heaven.*

46 *"become a,"* Perry, "Owsley and Me."

46 *"little ostentatiously,"* Perry e-mail, 11/18/2015.

46 *"Bay Area,"* ibid.

46 *"their accomplishments,"* ibid.

47 *"two-dimensional,"* Perry, "Owsley and Me."

47 *"Oh, that's right,"* ibid.

6. Pranksters and Angels

50 *"Go back to,"* http://www.lib.berkeley.edu/MRC/pacificaviet.html.

51 *"to be the,"* Gans, *Conversations with the Dead.*

51 *"Before I got,"* Bear e-mail, 4/1/2007.

52 *"was sort of,"* Eisner, "Interview with an Alchemist."

52 *"was the kind,"* Gans, *Conversations with the Dead.*

52 *"a bunch of,"* Bear interview, 1/31/2007.

52 *"Two hundred,"* Ibid.

53 *"a cross,"* Thompson, *Hell's Angels.*

53 *"massive arms,"* ibid.

53 *"about that,"* ibid.

53 *"the worthless,"* ibid.

54 *"Terry the Tramp,"* Bear interview, 1/31/2007.

54 *"There I was,"* ibid.

54 *"wolves were,"* ibid.

55 *"a lot more,"* ibid.

55 *"to go to,"* Bear e-mail, 4/1/2007.

7. Trips Festival

58 *"There were,"* McNally, *A Long Strange Trip.*

58 *"It was,"* Graham and Greenfield, *Bill Graham Presents.*

59 *"We were,"* ibid.

59 *"It was,"* Bear interview, 9/28/1989.

60 *"down the,"* McNally, *A Long Strange Trip.*

60 *"first sort of,"* Weir interview, 2/27/2007.

61 *"like a,"* Lesh, *Searching for the Sound.*

61 *"an Aussie,"* ibid.

61 *"every inch,"* ibid.

61 *"So, you're,"* ibid.

61 *"the result,"* ibid.

62 *"He said,"* Bear e-mail, 4/1/2007.

62 *"Other than,"* Lesh, *Searching for the Sound.*

62 *"like being,"* McNally, *A Long Strange Trip.*

62 *"Phil was,"* Bear interview, 1/31/2007.

62 *"That was,"* Scully interview, 3/2/2007.

63 *"extraordinarily ugly,"* McNally, *A Long Strange Trip.*

63 *"never heard,"* ibid.

63 *"the Dead,"* Bear interview, 12/4/1995.

63 *"Owsley saw,"* Scully interview, 3/2/2007.

64 *"So I,"* ibid.

65 *"something that,"* Gans, *Conversations with the Dead.*

65 *"about four,"* ibid.

65 *"a little,"* ibid.

65 *"two channels,"* ibid.

65 *"Owsley brought,"* Scully interview, 3/2/2007.

66 *"It was,"* Lesh, *Searching for the Sound.*

8. LA Fadeaway

67 *"We were,"* Bear interview, 1/31/2007.

68 *"It wasn't,"* ibid.

68 *"The Voice,"* Scully interview, 3/2/2007.

69 *"This is,"* McNally, *A Long Strange Trip.*

70 *"a hippie,"* ibid.

70 *"obviously a,"* ibid.

70 *"was both,"* Weir interview, 2/27/2007.

70 *"We'd met,"* Graham and Greenfield, *Bill Graham Presents.*

70 *"The band,"* ibid.

70 *"was as,"* Kreutzmann with Eisen, *Deal.*

71 *"had Phil's,"* McNally, *A Long Strange Trip.*

71 *"a combination,"* ibid.

71 *"I'll tell,"* Bear interview, 1/31/2007.

71 *"something else,"* ibid.

71 *"saw sound,"* ibid.

72 *"He came,"* Scully interview, 3/2/2007.

73 *"We all had,"* Bear interview, 1/31/2007.

74 *"Look what,"* Tendler and May, *Brotherhood of Eternal Love.*

74 *"the bit,"* Bear e-mail, 4/1/2007.

74 *"I remember,"* Weir interview, 2/27/2007.

75 *"We were,"* Perry e-mail, 11/6/2015.

9. Olompali

78 *"only out,"* Bear interview, 12/4/1995.

78 *"The Bear,"* Weir interview, 2/27/2007.

78 *"Owsley liked,"* Scully interview, 3/2/2007.

78 *"some bigger,"* Bear c-mail, 4/1/2007.

79 *"It never,"* Reich and Wenner, *Garcia.*

79 *"They decided,"* Bear interview, 12/4/1995.

79 *"He gave,"* McNally interview, 2/28/2007.

10. Print the Legend

82 *"flying on LSD,"* Stevens, *Storming Heaven.*

82 *"heaping pile,"* Reasons, " 'Mr. LSD' Makes Millions."

83 *"running,"* ibid.

83 *"he had,"* ibid.

83 *"even Owsley's,"* ibid.

83 *"What kind,"* ibid.

83 *"dropped from,"* ibid.

83 *"with all,"* ibid.

83 *"Home Made Drugs,"* San Francisco Chronicle, October 5, 1966.

84 *"I vaguely,"* Weir interview, 2/27/2007.

84 *"We were,"* Bear interview, 3/18/1997.

85 *"revered because,"* Scully interview, 3/2/2007.

85 *"the high,"* Greenfield, *Timothy Leary.*

86 *"Somebody played,"* ibid.

86 *"flick on,"* ibid.

86 *"the rest,"* ibid.

86 *"Are you,"* ibid.

86 *"Everything Tim,"* ibid.

87 *"Unless you,"* Greenfield, *Timothy Leary.*

87 *"Leary may,"* Perry, "Owsley and Me."

87 *"The clear,"* Wolfe, *Electric Kool-Aid Acid Test.*

88 *"they made,"* Gissen Stanley with Davis, *Owsley and Me.*

89 *"We spent,"* Bear interview, 3/18/1997.

90 *"I stopped,"* ibid.

90 *"the most,"* Bear e-mail, 4/6/2007.

91 *"Robin Goodfellow,"* Stevens, *Storming Heaven.*

91 *"I literally,"* Bear e-mail, 4/6/2007.

92 *"Owsley habitually,"* Perry e-mail, 12/16/2015.

93 *"Mr. LSD,"* Dorson, *America in Legend.*

93 *"Anecdotal legends,"* ibid.

94 *"groove,"* ibid.

94 *"Owsley represents,"* ibid.

94 *"All myths,"* Rogers, "Haight-Ashbury Era's Owsley Stanley."

94 *"I've been,"* Bear interview, 1/31/2007.

94 *"lived with,"* Barlow interview, 3/3/2007.

95 *"thinking exactly,"* ibid.

95 *"Owsley said,"* ibid.

95 *"various people,"* ibid.

96 *"You become,"* ibid.

11. Monterey Pop, and Beyond

97 *"drice,"* ibid.

99 *"working around,"* ibid.

100 *"Bobby Dylan,"* Perry, "Owsley and Me."

100 *"Hi, Bob,"* Perry e-mail, 10/27/2015.

100 *"Now, at,"* Graham and Greenfield, *Bill Graham Presents.*

101 *"But it,"* ibid.

101 *"I sent,"* Bear e-mail, 4/1/2007.

12. Getting Busted

105 *"It was,"* Graham and Greenfield, *Bill Graham Presents.*

106 *"collapsed into,"* Perry, "Owsley and Me."

107 *"the acid,"* von Hoffman, *We Are the People.*

107 *"The change,"* Bear e-mail, 4/1/2007.

107 *"My regular,"* Bear interview, 1/31/2007.

107 *"the money,"* Bear e-mail, 4/6/2007.

107 *"feel it,"* ibid.

108 *"did not,"* ibid.

108 *"border policemen,"* Perry, "Owsley and Me."

108 *"cops don't,"* ibid.

108 *"a regular,"* ibid.

108 *"Persian rugs,"* ibid.

109 *"a regular,"* ibid.

109 *"an ordinary,"* Bear e-mail, 4/1/2007.

109 *"All that,"* ibid.

110 *"panic in,"* "LSD 'Tycoon' Held."

110 *"to a,"* ibid.

110 *"How did,"* "Owsley Guilty."

110 *"made the,"* ibid.

110 *"actually a,"* "LSD 'Tycoon' Held."

110 *"gives the,"* ibid.

13. Two Festivals

113 *"a clubhouse,"* McNally, *A Long Strange Trip.*

113 *"I worked,"* Bear interview, 12/4/1995.

114 *"the definitive,"* *Live at the Carousel Ballroom 1968.*

115 *"would never,"* Graham and Greenfield, *Bill Graham Presents.*

115 *"decided to,"* ibid.

115 *"nobody injected,"* ibid.

116 *"He was,"* ibid.

116 *"I always,"* Bear e-mail, 4/1/2007.

117 *"We used,"* Browne, *So Many Roads.*

117 *"As soon,"* Bear interview, 9/28/1989.

118 *"We're doing,"* McNally, *A Long Strange Trip.*

118 *"I never,"* Bear interview, 1/31/2007.

119 *"sightless as,"* Lydon, "Good Old Grateful Dead."

119 *"we can,"* ibid.

119 *"righteous,"* ibid.

119 *"still lost,"* ibid.

119 *"Listen, are,"* ibid.

120 *"A good night,"* ibid.

120 *"What's so,"* ibid.

120 *"sleepy but,"* ibid.

120 *"like two,"* ibid.

122 *"You sonofabitch!,"* Scully with Dalton, *Living with the Dead.*

122 *"I will,"* Gissen Stanley with Davis, *Owsley and Me.*

122 *"really did,"* Jackson, *Goin' down the Road.*

122 *"He was,"* Browne, *So Many Roads.*

122 *"I talked,"* Bear interview, 9/28/1989.

122 *"a lot of,"* http://www.thebear.org/GDLogo.html.

123 *"spend a,"* ibid.

123 *"was a,"* ibid.

123 *"perhaps the,"* ibid.

123 *"Oh, that's,"* Bear interview, 1/31/2007.

123 *"a few,"* http://www.thebear.org/GDLogo.html.

123 *"I didn't,"* Bear interview, 1/31/2007.

124 *"would rank,"* McNally, *Long Strange Trip.*

124 *"We arrived,"* Bear interview, 12/4/1995.

124 *"hooked ropes,"* ibid.

124 *"out came,"* ibid.

124 *"and there,"* ibid.

125 *"It's nice,"* McNally, *A Long Strange Trip.*

125 *"The wrong,"* Bear e-mail, 1/31/2007.

125 *"the brown acid,"* www.hark.com/clips/ygmhswwswk-brown-acid-warning.

126 *"seemed to,"* "Owsley Guilty."

126 *"They found,"* Scully interview, 3/2/2007.

127 *"I knew,"* Bear interview, 9/28/1989.

128 *"We looked,"* ibid.

128 *"took just,"* ibid.

129 *"the Pearl,"* Graham and Greenfield, *Bill Graham Presents.*

129 *"the most,"* ibid.

129 *"wore more,"* ibid.

129 *"loaded to,"* ibid.

129 *"Gettin' smaller,"* ibid.

14. Set Up Like a Bowling Pin

133 *"Look, you,"* "Police in the Big Easy."

133 *"a pound,"* McNally, *A Long Strange Trip.*

133 *"Rock Musicians,"* *New Orleans Times-Picayune.*

133 *"The promoter,"* Bear interview, 1/31/2007.

134 *"a tiny,"* "Owsley Stanley Serves Time."

134 *"a threat,"* ibid.

134 *"accepted that,"* Gissen Stanley with Davis, *Owsley and Me.*

134 *"refused to,"* ibid.

135 *"Notes on,"* ibid.

136 *"At Terminal,"* Bear interview, 1/31/2007.

137 *"I had,"* Gans, *Conversations with the Dead.*

138 *"just great,"* Reich and Wenner, *Garcia.*

139 *"When I,"* Bear interview, 1/31/2007.

139 *"of my,"* Perry, "Owsley and Me."

139 *"a lion's,"* ibid.

139 *"all sorts,"* ibid.

139 *"The joke,"* ibid.

140 *"word was,"* ibid.

140 *"something funny,"* ibid.

140 *"in his,"* ibid.

140 *"Publius,"* ibid.

141 *"completely changed,"* Browne, *So Many Roads.*

141 *"The scene,"* Barlow interview, 3/3/2007.

141 *"The thing,"* Bear interview, 12/4/1995.

142 *"three really,"* Lesh, *Searching for the Sound.*

142 *"the supremo,"* ibid.

142 *"the wild-eyed,"* ibid.

142 *"each of,"* ibid.

142 *"there was,"* Weir interview, 2/27/2007.

142 *"I found,"* Bear e-mail, 4/1/2007.

143 *"I'm used,"* McNally, *A Long Strange Trip.*

143 *"I said,"* Bear interview, 1/31/2007.

144 *"here's a,"* ibid.

144 *"He wanted,"* McNally interview, 2/28/2007.

15. Wall of Sound

145 *"Bear had,"* Barlow interview, 3/3/2007.

147 *"I was,"* Greenfield, *Dark Star.*

148   *"I had,'"* Bear interview, 1/31/2007.

149   *"kept shifting,"* Bear interview, 12/4/1995.

149   *"a single,"* ibid.

150   *"not merely,"* McNally, *A Long Strange Trip.*

150   *"piloting a,"* ibid.

151   *"as flat,"* Kreutzmann with Eisen, *Deal.*

151   *"Owsley's brain,"* ibid.

151   *"impossible to,"* ibid.

151   *"The Wall,"* Bear interview, 12/4/1995.

151   *"The Wall,"* Weir interview, 2/27/2007.

152   *"had no,"* Bear interview, 12/4/1995.

16. Growing Weed

153   *"better gigs,"* McNally, *A Long Strange Trip.*

153   *"Egypt or,"* ibid.

153   *"There's,"* Graham and Greenfield, *Bill Graham Presents.*

154   *"When they,"* Bear interview, 1/31/2007.

154   *"I got,"* ibid.

155   *"They were,"* ibid.

155   *"Sure enough,"* ibid.

156   *"who was,"* ibid.

156   *"I did,"* ibid.

157   *"One of,"* ibid.

158   *"So here,"* ibid.

158   *"When you,"* ibid.

158   *"We armed,"* ibid.

159   *"But there,"* ibid.

159   *"I have,"* ibid.

17. Bear's Dream

161   *"I was,"* McNally interview, 2/28/2007.

164 *"as if,"* Bear interview, 9/28/1989.

164 *"weird dream,"* ibid.

164 *"I said,"* ibid.

165 *"Then I,"* ibid.

165 *"Noaa is,"* ibid.

166 *"I got,"* ibid.

166 *"When you,"* ibid.

167 *"When this,"* ibid.

167 *"on an airplane,"* Barlow interview, 3/3/2007.

168 *"a ninety,"* Gans, *Conversations with the Dead.*

18. The Land Down Under

169 *"a reticulated,"* Bear interview, 1/31/2007.

171 *"I told,"* ibid.

171 *"I said,"* ibid.

171 *"a sort of,"* Weir interview, 2/27/2007.

172 *"looking like,"* Bear interview, 1/31/2007.

172 *"He was,"* Barlow interview, 3/3/2007.

173 *"The way,"* conversation with John Perry Barlow, 1/26/16.

173 *"I always,"* Bear interview, 1/31/2007.

174 *"He was,"* author interview, 2007.

175 *"He had,"* ibid.

175 *"I don't,"* ibid.

175 *"Hey, Bear,"* ibid.

175 *"Bobby, you,"* ibid.

176 *"Get your,"* ibid.

177 *"I've had,"* Bear interview, 1/31/2007.

19. Real Love

179 *"He was,"* Sheilah Manning Stanley interview, 3/14/2015.

180 *"Spencer Dryden,"* Graham and Greenfield, *Bill Graham Presents.*

180 *"seemed very,"* Sheilah Manning Stanley interview, 3/14/2015.

180 *"came upon,"* ibid.

181 *"Not particularly,"* ibid.

181 *"In Australia,"* ibid.

182 *"Bear came,"* Ibid.

183 *"The party,"* Bear interview, 1/31/2007.

183 *"Redbird was,"* Sheilah Manning Stanley interview, 3/14/2015.

184 *"What happened,"* Bear interview, 12/4/1995.

186 *"Sheilah is,"* Bear e-mail, 4/2/2007.

20. Old and in the Way

187 *"a blockage,"* Bear interview, 1/31/2007.

187 *"the best,"* ibid.

187 *"They did,"* ibid.

188 *"I now,"* ibid.

188 *"Bear would,"* Barlow interview, 3/3/2007.

189 *"It was,"* Gissen Stanley with Davis, *Owsley and Me.*

190 *"already read,"* ibid.

190 *"If you're,"* ibid.

190 *"If you,"* ibid.

191 *"and a,"* ibid.

191 *"a Pegasus,"* ibid.

191 *"the family,"* ibid.

191 *"You're a,"* ibid.

192 *"a perfect,"* Ibid.

192 *"Both Starfinder,"* Bear interview, 1/31/2007.

193 *"stage four,"* Bear interview, ibid.

193 *"Normally within,"* ibid.

194 *"What they,"* ibid.

194 *"Half my,"* ibid.

195 *"All the,"* Sheilah Manning Stanley interview, 3/14/2015.

196 *"like you,"* Bear interview, 1/31/2007.

196 *"with a,"* ibid.

196 *"Every one,"* ibid.

196 *"By the,"* ibid.

197 *"Do you,"* ibid.

197 *"I think,"* ibid.

197 *"no clue,"* ibid.

197 *"I didn't,"* ibid.

21. A Visit from Bear

202 *"I've learned,"* Sheilah Manning Stanley, 5/31/2007.

202 *"But, hey,"* Bear, 5/31/2007.

203 *"Stress,"* Sheilah Manning Stanley, 5/31/2007.

205 *"Anytime,"* Selvin, "For the Unrepentant Patriarch."

205 *"there is,"* Bear interview, 1/31/2007.

205 *"everything exists,"* ibid.

22. On the Way Home

207 *"open discussion,"* www.entheogenesis.org.

207 *"Bear did,"* Sheilah Manning Stanley interview, 3/14/2015.

208 *"I was,"* ibid.

208 *"You know,"* ibid.

209 *"Hold on,"* ibid.

209 *"I want,"* ibid.

209 *"There was,"* ibid.

209 *"pandemonium at,"* ibid.

210 *"No, no,"* ibid.

210 *"Well, that's,"* ibid.

210 *"Suddenly after,"* ibid.

212 *"'Do you,'"* ibid.

212 "Was there," Hunter, "An Anthem for the Bear," www.reddit
.com/r/gratefuldead.

Epilogue: More Anthems for the Bear

215 *"Acid King,"* John Perry Barlow via Twitter, 3/13/2011.

215 *"He is,"* Barlow interview, 3/3/2007.

216 *"Bear, for,"* Phil Lesh, www.furthur.net.boards.

217 *"I never,"* Browne, "Dead Recall the Colorful Life."

217 *"I tend,"* Bear interview, 1/31/2007.

218 *"a profound,"* Markoff, *What the Dormouse Said.*

218 *"one of,"* ibid.

Appendix: Bear's Choice—a Selected Discography

221 *"enough money,"* Sheilah Manning Stanley interview, 3/14/2015.

222 *"rare recordings,"* www.owsleystanleyfoundation.org.

222 *"for the,"* ibid.

223 *"extra nice,"* www.thebear.org.

223 *"always secondary,"* ibid.

223 *"The demands,"* ibid.

224 *"had no,"* ibid.

224 *"The performance,"* ibid.

224 *"one I,"* ibid.

224 *"None of,"* https://cn.wikipedia.org/wiki/Steal_Your_Face.

225 *"wonderful opportunity,"* www.thebear.org.

225 *"capture a,"* ibid.

225 *"It was,"* ibid.

225 *"I didn't,"* ibid.

226 *"the two,"* ibid.

227 *"just in,"* ibid.

227 *"And yes,"* ibid.

227 *"This concert,"* ibid.

228 *"I have,"* ibid.

228 *"about 40%,"* ibid.

228 *"was able,"* ibid.

229 *"1969 was,"* ibid.

229 *"For me,"* ibid.

230 *"1972 saw,"* ibid.

230 *"Dick's Picks,"* liner notes, *Dick's Picks, Volume 36.*

231 *"a complete,"* www.thebear.org.

231 *"taken from,"* ibid.

231 *"to 'make,'"* ibid.

231 *"they must,"* ibid.

231 *"a small,"* ibid.

231 *"be hailed,"* ibid.

231 *"The sound,"* ibid.

231 *"This is,"* liner notes, *Live at the Carousel Ballroom 1968.*

232 *"I have,"* www.thebear.org.

Bibliography

Interviews

John Perry Barlow—3/3/2007.

Bear (Augustus Owsley Stanley III)—9/28/1989, 12/4/1995, 3/18/1997, 1/31/2007.

Dennis McNally—2/28/2007.

Rock Scully—3/2/2007.

Sheilah Manning Stanley—3/14/2015.

Bob Weir—2/27/2007.

Ron Wickersham—3/2/2007.

Books

Acid Dreams: The CIA, LSD, and the Sixties Rebellion, Martin A. Lee and Bruce Shlain, New York: Grove Press, 1985.

America in Legend: Folklore from the Colonial Period to the Present, Richard M. Dorson, New York: Pantheon Books, 1973.

Bill Graham Presents: My Life Inside Rock and Out, Bill Graham and Robert Greenfield, New York: Doubleday, 1992.

The Brotherhood of Eternal Love: From Flower Power to Hippie Mafia, Stewart Tendler and David May, London: Panther Books, 1984.

Captain Trips: A Biography of Jerry Garcia, Sandy Troy, New York: Thunder's Mouth Press, 1994.

Conversations with the Dead, David Gans, Secaucus, N.J.: Citadel Underground, 1993.

Dark Star: An Oral Biography of Jerry Garcia, Robert Greenfield, New York: William Morrow, 1996.

Deal: My Three Decades of Drumming, Dreams, and Drugs with the Grateful Dead, Bill Kreutzmann with Benjy Eisen, New York: St. Martin's Press, 2015.

The Electric Kool-Aid Acid Test, Tom Wolfe, New York: Farrar, Straus and Giroux, 1968.

Garcia, editors of *Rolling Stone*, New York: Little, Brown, a Rolling Stone Press Book, 1995.

Garcia: An American Life, Blair Jackson, New York: Viking Press, 1999.

Garcia: The Rolling Stone Interview, Charles Reich and Jann Wenner, San Francisco: Straight Arrow Books, 1972.

Goin' Down the Road: A Grateful Dead Traveling Companion, Blair Jackson, New York: Three Rivers Press, 1992.

The Haight-Ashbury: A History, Charles Perry, New York: Wenner Books, 2005.

Hell's Angels: The Strange and Terrible Saga of the Outlaw Motorcycle Gangs, Hunter Thompson, New York: Random House, 1967.

Intoxication: The Universal Drive for Mind-Altering Substances, Ronald K. Siegel, South Paris, Maine: Park Street Press, 1989, 2005.

Kentucky Profiles: Biographical Profiles in Honor of Holman Hamilton, edited by James C. Klotter and Peter J. Schillinger, Frankfort, Ky.: Kentucky Historical Society, 1982.

The Kybalion, The Three Initiates, Minneapolis, Minn.: Filiquarian Publishing, 2006.

Living with the Dead: Twenty Years on the Bus with Garcia and the Grateful Dead, Rock Scully with David Dalton, New York: Little, Brown, 1996.

A Long Strange Trip: The Inside History of the Grateful Dead, Dennis McNally, New York: Broadway Books, 2002.

LSD—My Problem Child, Albert Hofmann, New York: McGraw-Hill, 1980.

No Simple Highway: A Cultural History of the Grateful Dead, Peter Richardson, New York: St. Martin's Press, 2015.

Owsley and Me: My LSD Family, Rhoney Gissen Stanley with Tom Davis, Rhinebeck, N.Y.: Monkfish Book Publishing, 2012.

The Politics of Ecstasy, Timothy Leary, New York: G. P. Putnam's Sons, 1968.

The Rolling Stone Rock 'n' Roll Reader, edited by Ben Fong-Torres, New York: Bantam Books, 1974.

Searching for the Sound: My Life with the Grateful Dead, Phil Lesh, New York: Little, Brown, 2005.

Skeleton Key: A Dictionary for Deadheads, David Shenk and Steve Silberman, New York: Doubleday, 1994.

So Many Roads: The Life and Times of the Grateful Dead, David Browne, New York: Da Capo Press, 2015.

Storming Heaven, Jay Stevens, New York: Atlantic Monthly Press, 1987.

TiHKAL: The Continuation, Alexander Shulgin and Ann Shulgin, Berkeley, Calif.: Transform Press, 1997.

Timothy Leary: A Biography, Robert Greenfield, New York: Harcourt, 2006.

We Are the People Our Parents Warned Us Against, Nicholas von Hoffman, Lanham, Md.: Ivan R. Dee, 1988.

What the Dormouse Said: How the 60s Counterculture Shaped the Personal Computer Industry, John Markoff, New York: Viking, 2005.

The WPA Guide to Kentucky, compiled and written by the Federal Writers' Project of the Work Projects Administration for the State of Kentucky, Lexington: University Press of Kentucky, 1939.

Articles

"A. O. Stanley, Jr. to Run for Senate," *Lexington* (Ky.) *Herald*, 3/28/1968.

"The Dead Recall the Colorful Life of LSD Pioneer Owsley Stanley," David Browne, *Rolling Stone*, 3/30/2011.

"For the Unrepentant Patriarch of LSD, Long, Strange Trip Winds Back to Bay Area," Joel Selvin, *San Francisco Chronicle*, 7/12/2007.

"Good Old Grateful Dead," Michael Lydon, *Rolling Stone*, 8/23/1969.

"The Greying of the Groovers," Andrew Brown, *Guardian*, 5/28/1997.

"Haight-Ashbury Era's Owsley Stanley Finds Serenity in Sculpture, Sound," John Rogers, Associated Press, 5/24/1996.

"LSD 'Tycoon' Held After Orinda Raid," *San Francisco Chronicle*, 12/21/1967.

"'Mr. LSD' Makes Million Without Breaking the Law—Young Drug Manufacturer Wins 'Acid Head' Set's Applause After Following Checkered Career," George Reasons, *Los Angeles Times*, 10/3/1966.

"Owsley: A Danger to the Community," *Rolling Stone*, 4/16/1970.

"Owsley and Me," Charles Perry, *Rolling Stone*, 11/25/1982.

"Owsley Guilty: 67½ Righteous Grams," *Rolling Stone*, 11/15/1969.

"Owsley Stanley Serves Time," *Rolling Stone*, 9/17/1970.

"Police in the Big Easy Giving Bands a Hard Time," *Rolling Stone*, 3/7/1970.

"Researchers Dispute Ezra Pound's 'Insanity,'" Herbert Mitgang, *New York Times*, 10/3/1981.

"Rock Musicians, 'King of Acid' Arrested," *New Orleans Times-Picayune*, 1/31/1970.

"The Story of the Acid Profiteers," Mary Jo Worth, *Village Voice*, 8/22/1974.

Web Sites

"Augustus Owsley Stanley," McKenzie Martin, http://explorekyhistory.ky.gov.

"Interview with an Alchemist: Bear Owsley Interview," Bruce Eisner, May 17, 1998, http://www.bruceeisner.

www.entheogenesis.org.

www.furthur.net.boards.

www.hark.com/clips/.
www.historykygovenors.com/aostanley.htm.
www.ibiblio.org/hyperwar/USN/ships/.
www.owsleystanleyfoundation.org.
www.reddit.com/r/gratefuldead.
www.thebear.org.

E-mails

Bear (Augustus Owsley Stanley III)—1/31/2007, 3/27/2007, 4/1/2007, 4/2/2007, 4/6/2007, 4/13/2007, 4/16/2007, 4/21/2007, 4/27/2007, 7/1/2007.

Melissa Cargill—2/14/2007, 2/15/2007, 2/28/2007, 3/17/2007.

Charles Perry—106/3/2015, 6/4/2015, 6/6/2015, 6/7/2015, 6/8/2015, 6/12/2015, 10/16/2015, 10/27/2015, 11/6/2015, 11/18/2015, 12/16/2015.

Index